Praise for *Wedding Cake for Breakfast*

"If you want to smile, cry, laugh, grieve, or just plain nod knowingly in the face of newlywedded supposed-to-b̶ⁱ̶ ̶ ̶ ̶ ̶ ̶ ̶ ̶ ̶ ̶ ̶ s your friend." —Laura Munson, autʰ᷉ ̶ ̶ ̶ ̶ ̶ ̶ ̶ ̶ ̶ ̶ ̶ ̶ ̶ ̶ ̶ *k It Is*

"These insightful essays offer ̶ ̶ ̶ ̶ ̶ ̶ ̶ ̶ ̶ ̶ ̶ ̶ ̶ ̶ pect from a collection about the fiᵣ ̶ ̶ ̶ ̶ ̶ ̶ ̶ ̶ ̶ ̶ you treat yourself to *Wedding Cake for ̶ ̶ ̶ ̶ ̶*, you will come away entertained, encouraged, and enlightened, as if you'd just spent a weekend in the company of dear friends."

—Therese Fowler, author of *Souvenir* and *Exposure*

"*Wedding Cake for Breakfast* is a pure delight! What a wonderful reminder that in the end we are *all* neurotic, scared, and somewhat delirious as we navigate that often wacky but usually happy first year of marriage." —Jessica Anya Blau, author of *Drinking Closer to Home*

"I loved *Wedding Cake* so much, I just couldn't put it down! I highly recommend this delightful and delightfully frank look at marriage in its blush of infancy (aka before the dysfunction kicks in). Men: if you want to understand your bride, read this book. It pulls the curtain back to reveal the fertile imagination lurking in the female mind."

—Jenny Gardiner, author of *Slim to None*

"*Wedding Cake for Breakfast* is a perfectly rendered collection of wise and funny memories about the exquisitely complex first year of marriage. Simmering with love and powered by talented writers who paint hope and heart into every story, this book should be required reading for anyone who has or is about to tie the knot."

—Ann Wertz Garvin, author of *On Maggie's Watch*

WEDDING CAKE
for BREAKFAST

Essays on the Unforgettable First Year of Marriage

Edited by KIM PEREL
and WENDY SHERMAN

BERKLEY BOOKS, NEW YORK

BERKLEY BOOKS
Published by the Penguin Group
Penguin Group (USA) Inc.
375 Hudson Street, New York, New York 10014, USA
Penguin Group (Canada), 90 Eglinton Avenue East, Suite 700, Toronto, Ontario M4P 2Y3, Canada (a division of Pearson Penguin Canada Inc.) • Penguin Books Ltd., 80 Strand, London WC2R 0RL, England • Penguin Group Ireland, 25 St. Stephen's Green, Dublin 2, Ireland (a division of Penguin Books Ltd.) • Penguin Group (Australia), 250 Camberwell Road, Camberwell, Victoria 3124, Australia (a division of Pearson Australia Group Pty. Ltd.) • Penguin Books India Pvt. Ltd., 11 Community Centre, Panchsheel Park, New Delhi—110 017, India • Penguin Group (NZ), 67 Apollo Drive, Rosedale, Auckland 0632, New Zealand (a division of Pearson New Zealand Ltd.) • Penguin Books (South Africa) (Pty.) Ltd., 24 Sturdee Avenue, Rosebank, Johannesburg 2196, South Africa

Penguin Books Ltd., Registered Offices: 80 Strand, London WC2R 0RL, England

This is an original publication of the Berkley Publishing Group.

The publisher does not have any control over and does not assume any responsibility for author or third-party websites or their content.

Copyright © 2012 by Kim Perel and Wendy Sherman
A continuation of this copyright page appears on page 254.
Cover design by Diana Kolsky
"Readers Guide" copyright © 2012 by Penguin Group (USA) Inc.
Cover photo: "Couple" © Heather Landis / Getty Images
Book design by Laura K. Corless

PUBLISHING HISTORY
Berkley trade paperback edition / May 2012

Library of Congress Cataloging-in-Publication Data

Wedding cake for breakfast : essays on the unforgettable first year of marriage / edited by Kim Perel and Wendy Sherman.
p.   cm.
ISBN 978-0-425-24730-3
1. Marriage.   2. Newlyweds.   I. Perel, Kim.   II. Sherman, Wendy.
HQ734.W426 2012
306.8—dc23
2011043949

PRINTED IN THE UNITED STATES OF AMERICA

10 9 8 7 6 5 4 3 2 1

Penguin is committed to publishing works of quality and integrity.
our readers;
e the authors' alone.

ALWAYS LEARNING   PEARSON

For my grandparents who, altogether,
have been married 120 years total and counting.

For my mom who taught me how to live,
and for my dad who taught me how to love.

—KIM PEREL

For Samantha and Alexandra.
You are my everything.

—WENDY SHERMAN

Contents

Contents

Introduction

We fell in love over half-eaten club sandwiches. Not with each other, but with an idea. Framed in the window of a cozy, if slightly cramped, West Village café on Bedford Street, two agents and an editor met for lunch to discuss the business of literature, and ended up talking for hours about life and relationships—the stuff of literature. In the glow of the window's tiny, twinkling lights, Wendy, Andie, and I discovered that we had each circled around a similar book concept: a collection that would pay tribute to the exhilarating and unpredictable first year of marriage.

As we sipped coffee from oversize mugs and watched bearded bicyclists and yellow cabs roll down the cobblestone streets, Andie told us that in the first year of her marriage, the same year the economy collapsed, her husband was laid off from his job. Though their early months of marriage weren't comprised of the lighter, furniture-buying days she'd imagined, she explained how she and her husband adjusted, and together found a new normal.

Possessed by the human (and often female) impulse to share, I talked about a couple I knew who wound up in a long-distance marriage for the first six months after their wedding, seeing each other only on weekends after long flights and taxing workweeks. Then Wendy told us about a friend of hers whose husband was diagnosed with a rare illness in their first married year; a year her friend spent sitting in hospital waiting rooms filled with the worst kind of anticipation. We all agreed the term *honeymoon period* was a misnomer.

In all the stories we told, it seemed that each of the couples dealt with real life so suddenly after the headiness of their matrimony that it was like coming down from a drug. Both man and wife had handled obstacles like illness and money troubles before marriage, but never as a lawfully wedded couple. Now it all held more gravity—there was a future to imagine, new families to be considered, a marriage to uphold. Though for all the couples we discussed it seemed that, instead of becoming distant, they got stronger, and only held on to each other more tightly.

As the restaurant emptied, I told them about another close friend of mine. She was an obsessive, creative type with a stubborn streak and a tendency toward grand ideas that were nearly impossible to execute; a somewhat lethal personality cocktail to have when planning a wedding. In preparation for her nuptials, this friend ensured that every bead on her dress, every note the band played, and every flower petal fit into the aesthetic vision she had of her *Big Day*. The result was a gorgeous logistical quagmire of a wedding that left her guests feeling a mixture of bliss and exhaustion in its wake.

A group of us celebrated with the couple after the wedding and stayed over in a Lower East Side hotel. In the morning, I went over to my friend's bridal suite to ask the newlyweds what they had planned for breakfast, and found the couple in the living room area hunched over an open cake box. Ravaged and topped with melting white icing, their once-pristine red velvet wedding cake looked like a tiny mass of snowcapped mountains. "I was so busy at the wedding I didn't get to try the cake," my friend admitted.

I watched as she and her husband spent the first morning of their marriage side by side on the sofa with the top tier of their wedding cake on their laps, shoveling dollops of cream-cheese frosting and crimson cake into their mouths with flimsy plastic utensils.

"I can't believe you two are married," I said. I turned to my friend. "What are you going to do now that you don't have to plan the wedding of the century?" It was a playful jab, but she and her husband's faces seemed to dissolve. Perhaps it was the fact that they were twenty-five years old, or that they hadn't planned for anything but appetizers and invitations in the past year, but swap out the hotel couch for the back of a bus and their expressions were eerily similar to those of Ben and Elaine at the end of *The Graduate*.

Freeze-frame that expression. That, we decided, is where our book starts.

The essays you're about to read pick up after the Hollywood ending, when a man has already thrown rocks at a bedroom window to win over a woman, or someone has already run through the airport and begged the other person not to leave. Of course, so many Hollywood movies are contrived with dramatic emotional swells because the everyday grind doesn't have quite the same cinematic appeal. Love stories usually end with weddings instead of beginning with them. That's why, despite the more complex circumstances surrounding the marriages that inspired this book idea, we imagined a continuation of those romantic storylines, essays filled with sitcom-esque gaffes, perfect narrative arcs, and voyeuristic allure. We envisioned newly married couples having playful squabbles over how much (or how little) sex to have, run-ins with overbearing but well-meaning mother-in-laws, and witticisms about messy bathrooms, which would be, I'm ashamed to admit: *cute*. Instead, this book took on a life of its own with stories that were raw, wonderful, and strange all at once, proving that the days devoid of melodrama are the truly rich ones and that strong writers don't need the will-they-won't-they high-stakes marriage at the end of their stories to be captivating and moving, only the everyday complications of the modern marriage and the quiet angst of ordinary domestic life.

In her poignant essay "Shared Anniversary," native New Yorker Daphne Uviller remembers her beautiful ceremony alongside the horror of 9/11, but while her wedding date will always be too close to tragedy for comfort, she realizes that she can hold on to her husband when the ground beneath them is splitting. Other essays are quirky, like Abby Sher's "Juan and Marita," in which the author imagines her hand-me-down cake toppers as stand-ins for her deceased parents, like guardian angels fashioned from Play-Doh. She reveals how giving away those cake toppers amplified her loss, as she built a new life without her parents in that first year. Darcie Maranich is achingly candid about the reality of her husband's return from deployment and how difficult it was to bring him back into the family fold. Meanwhile, Sarah Pekkanen explores the change in family dynamics that marriage creates with an essay about how her mother was terrified of losing her daughter to her in-laws, fearing that she would somehow disappear into her new husband's family. Amy Wilson ruminates on what it means when married couples fight, while Sophie Littlefield cautions against what can happen when couples pretend nothing is wrong. Others, like Cathy Alter's "Ciao Baggage," a story about losing luggage on a trip to Italy with her husband, and realizing that love is more important than clean underwear, offer levity.

Lines like Andrea Collier's "the first year is the thing you have to get through to get to the marriage part" felt like sage advice, whereas

Susan Shapiro disclosed thoughts most women would keep to themselves. Candid admissions like those in Susan's essay, "The Last Honeymoon," in which she finds herself secretly fantasizing about being on her tropical paradise honeymoon with an old flame, would be taboo among friends in the thick of that heated first year, but in these pages she is free to divulge.

So while we weren't exactly sure what subject matters might be broached in the anthology, we did know that we wanted to provide our authors with a great deal of latitude. That's why we had only one stipulation: that the essays take place within that pivotal first year of marriage. We wanted to allow for the widest possible creative space for each writer to express (or confess) how she genuinely felt when her marriage was in its infancy, and we were curious to line up the snapshots of women in the first year of their together-forever lives and see what truths might develop.

I say snapshots because we're not tackling the first year of marriage in its entirety in this book. We know that modern marriage is more disparate than ever from one couple to the next, so we wanted to gather as many different pictures as possible. At the wedding, the snapshots are clear and these days there are so many photos taken of the bride and groom that the entire event can practically be reconstructed through time-lapse photography. In those pictures, everyone is smiling and gesturing, and the bride is wearing more concealer on her face than ever before. It's usually quite obvious what a wedding and a bride look like. But the prompting photographer is conveniently absent when that first fight happens or when the couple realizes that they each had different ideas about sightseeing on their honeymoon, or how to spend the wedding money they were gifted. The picture of what a wedding looks like is defined and recognizable, while the portrait of a married couple is blurrier, taking more time to come into focus.

Since marriage looks different to everyone, it's hard to know exactly how to reconcile both your concepts of "home" or "how married people act." In all of these stories, it seemed that the connective tissue running through them was that you learn as you go and eventually figure out the couple you'd like to be—because no one knows exactly how to be married at first.

That's why, in the most optimistic of worlds, when we finished editing the essays, I hoped for a collection to which married women could relate. What I was surprised to find was that I, too, could relate. I'm not married and I never have been, but I saw pieces of myself (and my past relationships) in each of these essays, and my hope is that you too will find pieces of yourself all throughout this collection, too.

By the time we organized the essays, the book felt like one interconnected journey and we wanted a singular cover image to capture that. What our brilliant designer, Diana, came up with was an artful portrayal of two newlyweds trying to keep their heads above water. You can't see the looks on their respective faces, so you don't know if they look stupefied by the vast ocean of decisions, compromises, and obstacles that lie before them—like my friends seemed that morning—or if they're wearing brave smiles. I think their expressions depend on your own outlook, though I like to envision that either way they're in it together, holding each other's hand.

WE WILL FIGURE IT OUT

Do You Want Fries with That?

SUSAN JANE GILMAN

I was not at all nervous the day I got married. I had no second thoughts, no Bridezilla meltdown, no last-minute panic in a parking lot. I walked myself down the aisle serenely. Feminist that I was, I wanted to make it clear that I was giving myself away, thank you—and of my own joyful volition. Standing beside the man who was now my husband, the Amazing Bob, I felt confident, radiant, and preternaturally calm.

It was only the day after the wedding that I turned into an absolute lunatic.

When the clerk at our hotel said, "Would you like me to put this on your credit card or you husband's?" I nearly had a seizure.

"My husband? Who the hell is that?"

Then I realized she meant Bob. "Oh My Fucking God," I said, turned to him. "You're my HUSBAND?"

I was like Helen Keller's dimwit cousin: my hand might've been under the water pump, but good luck getting me to grasp any connection between the words and reality: *Married. Wife. Husband.* For the first few days of our honeymoon, I kept glancing at Bob as he dozed on his beach chair. "Can you believe we're actually MARRIED?" I said, nudging him awake. "Like FOR REAL?"

"Um, yeah," Bob said. "Remember that big party we just had? Where you dressed up as a bride . . ."

At first, "being married" was a novelty: 3-D glasses, an Imperial yo-yo. But quickly, panic set in. Because "being married," I realized, really meant only one thing: I was now that much closer to getting divorced.

My parents were divorced. All my uncles and aunts were divorced. The Gilman Family marital track record had a 100 percent default rate. Growing up, I'd watched my mother rage through the house, slamming her fist down on the dinner table in frustration, my father turning gray and withdrawing from her more and more until his personality seemed to disappear entirely. Doors banging; daily resentments, betrayals, and nastiness; my cousins shuttled around under custody arrangements; my aunt and uncle arguing about money. I'd witnessed this corrosive unhappiness for years. When my parents finally separated after their twenty-sixth wedding anniversary, I vowed to myself: *That's it. I'm never getting married.*

But then, the Amazing Bob arrived: a stunningly cerebral, handsome man equally capable of immense kindness and smart-assed wit. What's more, he was at least as cynical as I was. Neither of us really believed in the institution of marriage. And yet, over time, it became clear that we were far better together than apart. We loved each other profoundly. We wanted all the tools available to take care of each other. And so we decided, finally, to take the plunge.

Albert Einstein, who was apparently also a very smart man, once observed, "Women marry men hoping they will change. Men marry women hoping they will not. So each is inevitably disappointed."

But Bob and I were already hip to this. We were in our thirties when we got engaged. Our student loans were paid off. The posters on our walls were framed. We could microwave popcorn without consulting the directions on the side of the package. Hell, we even read *The New York Review of Books*. We didn't expect an engagement ring or a marriage license to magically transform us. At best, we figured, wedlock would entitle us to better health insurance and maybe a new Cuisinart.

Yet, to our immense surprise, the evening that we exchanged our vows, Roman candles ignited within us. Standing together beneath our wedding canopy, I felt something akin to bliss.

The problem was: who in their right mind trusts bliss? During our honeymoon, Bob spooned me and fell asleep every night in a cloud of contentment, secure in the knowledge that we were now fully committed as husband and wife. I, on the other hand, lay blinking awake beside him having a full-blown anxiety attack. Surely, this "happy ending" of ours had to have a catch. Surely it was just a temporary reprieve—the gods teasing, "You want it? Psych!" Surely, tranquility was always just a precursor to some inevitable tragedy. As Bob breathed sweetly against my neck, I cataloged all the potential domestic catastrophes awaiting us.

Married. Husband. Wife. How could this possibly last? Never mind life's bigger traumas and losses: What if our love began to curdle, and all those qualities that once endeared us to each other—his bad puns, my histrionics—started to grate? What if we ended up eating our meals in tedious silence punctuated only by chewing and slurping? What if we became sexually indifferent? What if I became a slovenly, menopausal woman in a tracksuit while Bob started sprouting ear hair and dressing like Mr. Rogers? What if we started calling each other "Maw" and "Paw"? What if we became one of those couples who constantly indict each other, treating everyone else like a jury, saying stuff in public like: "My wife's idea of a 'balanced breakfast' is a donut and a martini—" "Oh really? Well, you'd drink, too, if you had a lover like Harry. Lemme tell you, an ATM transaction lasts longer than he does."

What if, every day that we spent together, a little part of us just died?

Overnight, I became an emotional hypochondriac—on alert for the slightest shifts in my husband's moods—convinced that it was only a matter of time before some terminal rot set in. IF I WASN'T VIGILANT AND PROACTIVE TWENTY-FOUR HOURS A DAY, I worried, OUR MARRIAGE WOULD DISINTEGRATE.

All those self-help books and triple-exclamation-point women's magazines I'd once mocked; suddenly I was scanning them in the supermarket for advice: Were Bob and I voicing our appreciation for each other daily? Were we having sex well above the national weekly average? How often were we laughing together? We were laughing, weren't we? Was I funny? Please, tell me I was funny. I wasn't worrying and second-guessing too much, was I? I took quizzes to find out.

I'd wake up sweaty and dry-mouthed. To preempt any domestic tedium, I became fixated, oddly, on tedious domestic things like tea lights and matching napkins. Every night when we got home from work, I decided, Bob and I had to have a candlelit cocktail hour—some wildly romantic "alone time" replete with toothpicks and breadsticks. I picked up smoked mackerel, pretentious imported cheese, herbed tofu spread, inedible candied kumquats. When Bob arrived home, he'd find a trayful of bizarre hors d'oeuvres on the coffee table alongside an opened bottle of Cabernet and a half-drunk wife.

"Well, well," he'd say bemusedly. "I see happy hour's already started."

"What do you mean by 'happy hour'?" I'd say anxiously, struggling to sit upright. "Are the other twenty-three we spend together miserable?"

Before I was married, I never bought lingerie. It was just glorified underwear; you were paying a lot of money for what was, essentially, string. Plus, the way guys carried on, fondling my breasts was like winning the lottery. So why, I wondered, should I knock myself out?

Now I went to Victoria's Secret. Most of their lingerie is designed to make women with modest or regular curves look curvier. But if you're curvy to begin with like me, you just look ridiculous. In the "Angel Collection," I looked nothing like Stephanie Seymour or Tyra Banks and everything like two grapefruits stuffed into a sweat sock. But I thought of my mother, the artist, in her tie-dyed leotards, funky head scarves, and hand-crocheted vests. My father often wished she'd dressed up more. I bought three aerodynamic lace push-up bras with tiny matching thongs. Bob didn't seem to mind—though he wasn't nearly as dazzled as I'd hoped he'd be. "Wow," was his reaction. "Can you breathe in that?"

Until my brother and I were in college, my parents didn't take a single weekend away together. By the time they began tromping grimly to Italy and San Francisco, they weren't on vacations so much as rescue missions. And so I began planning little post-honeymoon getaways for Bob and me, obsessively reading reviews of "romantic country inns" on the Internet. As soon as Bob walked in the door, I'd pepper him with questions: the Shenandoah Valley or Rehoboth? Beachfront or garden view? The Laura Ashley Room or the Beatrix Potter Suite?

I arranged for us to attend plays, film festivals, women's basketball games. I brought home porn. I baked cookies (okay: Pillsbury dough roll). I called Bob at work to see if there was any dry cleaning he needed me to pick up on my way home. Was he out of shaving cream? Should I rent a video? What did he think about ordering in sushi? Did he see the article on the latest climate change treaty? Had he heard the story about Eddie Izzard on National Public Radio? What was he thinking? How was he feeling? "How's your heart and soul?" I'd say. "Is everything okay? Just checking in."

In a matter of months, I'd gone from being the bestselling author of a book called *Kiss My Tiara: How to Rule the World as a Smart-Mouth Goddess* to a postmodern geisha who was essentially tromping around our apartment with a feather duster and a pair of bunny ears, hovering over my husband and chirping 24/7: "Do you want fries with that?"

It would be easy to argue that I was selling out my principles—or reverting to some supposedly "natural" female state of subservience. But my behavior, as I see it now, transcended all permutations of gender. It was rooted in something far more basic and universal: that desperate, overarching desire. *Please. Love me. Don't leave.*

Is it a surprise to anyone, however, that Bob was beginning to regard me not with increasing affection, but alarm? Love follows its own physics: the harder you try to attract, the stronger you repel. And yet I couldn't stop.

Finally, one Sunday morning, we sat together on the couch as we always did—he with his feet on the coffee table, me with my feet on his lap—sipping coffee and reading the *Times*—when I noticed: WE WERE BEING TOTALLY QUIET.

"Okay." I leapt to my feet. "This isn't working."

"What's not working?" said Bob, glancing up from the Week in Review section. "The newspaper?"

"All this silence," I cried, gesturing wildly. "We're just sitting here together on the couch. Reading. Without saying anything."

"Um, isn't that sort of how people read?"

"This isn't a LIBRARY. It's a MARRIAGE!" I shouted. "We should be making witty, intelligent conversation. We should be bantering like Spencer Tracy and Katharine Hepburn in *Woman of the Year*. We should be engaged in quick, policy-based repartee like the staff on *The West Wing*. We're smart. We're funny. Why the hell aren't we talking like them?"

"Well, for starters," Bob said slowly, "those characters you mentioned? They're fictional. And the reason they're funny and smart is because other people write their lines for them—"

"Stop being so goddamn calm and rational," I said. "Look at us! We're just SITTING HERE READING THE NEWSPAPER. We're married now. Shouldn't we be working at our relationship? Shouldn't we be having sex all the time? Shouldn't we at least be baring our souls to each other? I mean, is this what we're going to do? JUST SPEND THE REST OF OUR LIVES TOGETHER ON THE GODDAMN COUCH?"

Bob set down his newspaper and stared at me. "Okay, look," he said softly. He stood up and opened his arms. Reluctantly, I went to him. He drew me close and sighed. For a moment he didn't say anything. *This is it*, I thought. *He's going to divorce me*. Then he cleared his throat. His voice was gentle and slow.

"You know, any two people can have sex," he said. "And cracking jokes and being witty is great. But it's also work. And it's not real intimacy—"

I pulled back and looked at him. "So then let's talk with more intimacy," I said. "Every weekend, let's sit down, and discuss how our marriage is going, and if we're happy or not, and what our needs are, and what we think we can improve. We can call it our State of the Union address—"

"Suze." Bob took me by the shoulders and turned me to face him. "Stop, okay? You're trying too hard. Please. Don't try to manage my happiness."

"But—"

"Look." He gestured around the living room. "The way I see it, for two people just to snuggle on the couch, and read the Sunday paper together—in a way, that's more intimate than sex. Being quiet together—comfortably? That's real intimacy."

For a moment I just stared at him. Who the hell is this person? I thought. Is this guy really my HUSBAND? Where I came from, people were quiet only when they were seething or discontent, or when something was wrong and they wanted to punish each other.

My parents had dated for just two weeks before they'd gotten engaged. They were only twenty-three years old and still living at home with their parents. It had been a different era. In photographs from that time, they look so wondrous and trusting, so innocent. My creamy-skinned mother with her bouffant hair; my father, baby-faced, despite his posturing with a guitar. They'd had no compass, no sage counsel. No sooner did they get engaged than their families started to bicker and fight. Battle lines were drawn. My parents' modest wedding was a nightmare. Their fragile love was heartbreaking.

Still, I hadn't understood how they could've been married for twenty-six years and then—*poof*! The only way to make sense of their divorce was by assigning blame. Surely, my parents could've stayed together if only they'd just tried harder. If only they'd been more emotionally courageous and inventive. If only my mother had dressed more fashionably and my father had given her more thoughtful birthday gifts. If only they'd had sun-dried tomato spread and pita crisps together every evening and spent autumn weekends together in twee B&Bs. If only they'd gone to counseling sooner. If only they'd talked. If only. If only. If only.

My father had also read the paper every Sunday on our couch. But he'd read it alone, nervously barricaded behind the sports section. Feeling excluded and ignored, my mother fumed about the kitchen. "Why aren't you talking to me?" she'd snap. "Why don't you have anything interesting to say to me, huh? Where's your wit, your imagination? Why aren't we like Spencer Tracy and Katharine Hepburn?"

I'd forgotten this. Now I snuggled against Bob and started to cry. The candied kumquats, the unflattering lingerie, the forced cheeriness: had I been insane? "I'm sorry," I whispered. I was an accomplished career woman, a world traveler, an adult. Yet I still had so much to learn.

Bob looked at me. "It's okay. Just relax," he said softly, squeezing my shoulder. "Have a little faith."

Twinkie au Chocolat

ELIZABETH BARD

Imagine waking up every day next to a man who has never eaten a Twinkie. Such is the Faustian bargain I made when I moved to Paris and married my French husband in July of 2003.

My first year of marriage was also my first year of real life in France. My husband had seduced me with bloody steak, long walks through narrow cobblestone streets and wild-strawberry sorbet. Now there were bills, no central heating, and a makeshift kitchen with two electric burners in our tiny flat near the Canal Saint-Martin.

When you choose to marry into another culture, you have a lifetime of catching up to do. Gwendal had never seen *The Breakfast Club*, I had never seen *Les 400 Coups*. My first slow dance was to Wham. His was accompanied by some Italian pop star I had never heard of. But nowhere were our differences more pronounced than at the table, a spot we would be sharing, two or three meals a day—for the rest of our lives.

I grew up in 1970s New Jersey, drinking diet cream soda and eating instant mac 'n' cheese. The sex, drugs, and rock 'n' roll of my adolescence was a can of Pillsbury vanilla frosting and a plastic spoon. I spent weekends with my dad in New York City, learning to use chopsticks and, after a late movie, devouring pillowy cheese blintzes at the Kiev, an all-night Russian diner on Second Avenue. I knew a fish fork when I saw one, but might have told you potatoes grew on trees. My mother once asked an exterminator if squirrels laid eggs.

My husband, Gwendal, grew up in Saint-Malo, on the Channel coast of France. His father knew how to catch an eel with his bare hands. Gwendal carried pails of fresh milk, still warm and frothy with cream, ate crab apples from the tree in his grandfather's garden, and grew sick from devouring too many of the blackberries meant for jam. Until he was eleven, he thought broccoli was a made-up vegetable, invented, like cowboys and aliens, in the pages of his comic books.

We worshipped at different altars. To me, a family gathering was a Hebrew National salami and a fight over leftover lo mein for breakfast. Gwendal's memories of lingering family meals centered on the cheese plate (and a very bad experience with his father's stuffed cabbage). Cheese to me was flat, square, and fluorescent orange. For Gwendal, cheese was sacred, the closest thing the French have to a national religion. Every Christmas, his great-aunt Jane sent a discussize round of Saint-Nectaire through the mail. And every year, like a recitation of "The Night Before Christmas," I would hear the tale of the famous Noël Postal Strike of 1995. The postman arrived three weeks later with the package—oozing and pungent—held at arm's length.

Gwendal and I certainly had a different relationship to the fridge. The refrigerator in France is a utilitarian object, with strictly observed opening times, like banker's hours. In my house, the fridge was a humming center of activity; someone was always peeking in, grabbing something out, or looking for the leftover pork roast in a Ziploc baggie in the back. I found a full fridge reassuring, a princess surveying her realm. Sometimes Gwendal would find me just standing there, door open, eyeing the contents. "What are you doing?" he would ask, mystified. "Nothing," I said. Solving world peace. Choosing names for our unborn children. Just checking that the world is exactly as it should be.

Young married couples often talk about gaining weight together; true love's version of the "freshman fifteen." There were times when I felt like I was playing house, waiting for Gwendal to come home from work. Just before she died, my grandmother gave me her half aprons, frilly ones that you tie over a skirt to serve cocktails and finger sandwiches. If I'd had them during our first year of marriage, things might have taken a turn for the kinky. For a girl with a background in Renaissance bookbinding, but with no idea how to gut a fish, preparing a simple meal of whole mackerel sautéed in white wine felt like earning a graduate degree. Cooking became a liberating, creative enterprise, an MFA in *joie de vivre*.

During the early days of our marriage, I used food to welcome people, when my language skills weren't quite up to the task. With the most important parts of my personality amputated by my halting French, I was desperate to find another way to communicate. My husband's friends didn't know if I was intelligent, charming, witty, or warm. What they did know is that I made a mean sweet-potato puree and—after watching Gwendal a few times—a festive chicken, apricot, and coriander *tagine*.

There were times when I used the kitchen to hide. French dinner parties are marathons of cuisine and conversation, four or five hours—

and that's if no one is having a good time. If the people in question actually enjoy one another's company, you could be there all night. I remember those evenings; rapid-fire French buzzed in my ears, my brain felt foggy from the wine. It was easier to say, "I'm just going to check the roast" than "Dear God, I'm so bored and exhausted I'm considering sticking my head in the oven."

My husband and I are both only children, the sole inheritors of numerous family traditions, including recipes. A few weeks before the wedding, a set of neatly printed index cards arrived in the mail from Gwendal's grandmother Simone. Among the recipes were detailed instructions for Gwendal's favorite childhood dessert, *le bon jeune homme,* which he rapturously described to me as a carefully molded mountain of chocolate cream surrounded by a lake of crème anglaise. I glanced at the card; the first paragraph alone involved forty-five minutes of continuous stirring. The first time I made it, I burned the chocolate. The second time I stirred for an hour and ended up with chocolate milk. The third time, I cheated. Consulting Nigella Lawson's recipe for chocolate pots, I whisked in a solitary egg. My custard was firm to the touch, and no one was the wiser. Unmolding the chocolate mountain was simply too much pressure, so I served the chocolate custard in tall parfait glasses, topped with a layer of vanilla-flecked crème anglaise. Gwendal looked slightly disappointed, until he tasted it. Perhaps I would be worthy of carrying the torch after all.

I spoke a lot to my own grandmother that year. Like many Jewish Americans, my ancestors hailed from Eastern Europe—Minsk, Pinsk, or somewhere in between. I was hardly the first woman in my family to learn to cook in a new culture, a new city. My grandparents were married in 1941, and during the war my grandfather, an engineer, was sent to Utica, New York, to work in an aeronautics factory. My grand-mother learned to cook from the Italian ladies she met on line at the butcher. "Always use two kinds of meat," they told her. "Don't burn the garlic." "Dried parsley will do." The recipe that has come down to us is full of love and contradictions: a Jewish grandmother's spaghetti sauce full of juicy pork ribs.

Six months after our wedding, my father-in-law was diagnosed with stage-four colon cancer. I was helpless, and furious. I watched Gwendal and his mother navigate a medical system with excellent care, but no one to talk to. It was impossible to obtain more than a whispered diagnosis or any real discussion of treatment options. Unable to force the issue the way I would have in the United States— pitching a tent at the nurses' station, demanding to see the head of the department, the only place I could make myself useful was in the kitchen. My mother-in-law was surprisingly graceful in letting another woman take over her stove. I made simple things I'd learned from her: bags of baby scallops from the freezer, sautéed with diced onion, white wine, and a heaping tablespoon of crème fraîche. I pinched small amounts of sea salt from a ceramic jar my father-in-law, an art-ist, had made. The glaze was a deep blue mottled with gray tears, the lid sticky from kitchen grease. My mother sent over American mea-suring cups and bags of Domino's dark brown sugar, and I made batch after batch of chocolate-chip cookies. No pecans, dried cherries, or other fancy footwork was appropriate, just the recipe straight off the back of the Toll House bag. Even as his appetite faded, my father-in-law hoarded these cookies with a comic possessiveness, eat-ing them with tea during the long winter afternoons.

When I got homesick, and reruns of *The West Wing* would no

longer suffice, I would take a trip to Thanksgiving, a store in the Marais selling overpriced American imports. A package of Philadelphia cream cheese was seven dollars. Like Audrey Hepburn at Tiffany's, I would sweep my hands along the shelves of Pop-Tarts and raspberry fluff. I stopped to read the ingredients—something I would never do in the States—drinking in the comforting, polysyllabic beauty of it all.

Strangely enough, I never bought anything, not even a nostalgic can of Pillsbury vanilla frosting. It seemed wrong somehow, like eating *pho* in Bogotá—ne'er the twain shall meet. There were just too many wonderful things to eat in Paris to get stuck in my childhood obsession with partially hydrogenated soybean oil.

Thanksgiving itself—the holiday, that is—simply disappeared when I arrived in France. No one had the day off, or was plotting a 5 a.m. shopping spree to Best Buy for a forty-eight-foot flat-screen TV. Even if I had been linguistically capable of asking my butcher for a twenty-pound turkey, I suspect he would have laughed in my face. In any case, we didn't have an oven.

The Jewish holidays, in particular, took on a spectral, hidden presence. September in Paris is strolling weather. Walking along on our way to a movie, we saw men dressed in long black coats and wide-brimmed hats throwing bits of bread into the canal. In France, religion is meant to be completely absent from the public sphere, so it took me a moment to make the connection. The men were Orthodox Jews cleansing their sins in the water. And I had completely forgotten about Yom Kippur. I wondered how I had missed the holiday hustle bustle, even over the phone, and I was sad to discover there was nothing inside me that instinctively sprang to the surface on the day, even in a foreign land.

Food—and marriage, I would learn—represent an intimate comfort zone, a safe and loving space to expand your character, and occasionally a nest to retreat to when the world seems hostile and overwhelming. The summer after our wedding, I herniated a disc dragging a suitcase full of shoes through the streets of Paris. Hunched over and in pain, I wanted only one thing—take-out Chinese and a DVD of *Grease*. Gwendal tried to play along, hunched over on the edge of the sofa with his throwaway chopsticks and flimsy aluminum carton of pad thai. But the French are a civilized race. They prefer to eat meals at tables, with plates and napkins, and perhaps a glass of Bordeaux. On this point we would agree to disagree. I felt better than I had in weeks. I carefully flung my legs over the arm of the couch and laid my head in his lap. It was almost perfect. My kingdom for a Twizzler.

My husband and I will celebrate our ten-year wedding anniversary next year. Over time, our culinary habits have blended together. I am now a lover—and creator—of five-course French dinner parties, and Gwendal occasionally eats breakfast standing up at the kitchen counter. I still contemplate life's big questions in front of the open fridge. He still refuses to drink milk out of the container. C'est la vie.

Le Bon Jeune Homme
Chocolate Cream with Crème Anglaise

Adapted from Tante Jane Adam

I didn't muster the will to try this recipe until several years after our wedding. Is any man's childhood fantasy worth forty-five minutes of continuous stirring? Absolutely. Unmolding a mountain of wobbly chocolate cream seemed too risky, so I turned this into a black-and-white parfait, served in a tall glass. Gwendal looked slightly disappointed with the presentation, until he tasted it.

This is a great dinner party/holiday dessert—it looks terribly elegant, and because you must get it in the fridge the night before, there's less hassle on the day!

For the chocolate cream
> *1 egg*
> *6 oz dark chocolate (70 percent cocoa; I use Valrhona or Green & Black's)*
> *½ cup heavy cream*
> *½ cup whole milk*

For the crème anglaise
> *5 egg yolks*
> *⅓ cup sugar*
> *3 cups whole milk*
> *1 vanilla bean*
> *Fresh mint to garnish*

For the chocolate cream: Lightly beat the egg in a small bowl.

Chop the chocolate and place in the top of a double boiler with the cream and the milk. Heat, stirring to combine, until just below boiling. Turn off the heat.

Quickly whisk the beaten egg into the chocolate mixture until smooth. Divide the chocolate cream among 6 tall glasses. Refrigerate for at least 6 hours or overnight.

For the crème anglaise: In a medium mixing bowl, beat egg yolks with sugar until a light lemon yellow. Set aside.

Pour milk into a medium saucepan. Split the vanilla bean down the middle; scrape the seeds into the milk, and throw in the pod as well. Heat over a low flame, until just below boiling.

Slowly add the hot milk to the egg yolks, whisking continuously. Pour the mixture back into the saucepan and cook over low heat, stirring continuously, until the crème anglaise coats the back of a spoon, about 10 minutes.

Cool briefly in an ice bath; store in an airtight container in the fridge. Like the chocolate cream, this can be made a day ahead.

Just before serving, top the chocolate cream with a layer of crème anglaise and top with a sprig of mint.

SERVES 6–8

My Kitty-Corner Life

ANN HOOD

A week after we got married, my husband, Lorne, and I moved into a new apartment. All day we schlepped boxes and bags, furniture and clothes, across Providence. By eleven o'clock that night, I was too tired to unpack even one more dish, and my groom chivalrously offered to finish up. Happy and in love, I went to bed that night in our new queen-size bed with its wedding-gift, unslept-on sheets and comforter. I woke up to the smell of coffee brewing and the sounds of Lorne moving around. These heavy footsteps, this smell of shaving cream and Irish Spring soap, the tweeds and flannels peeking out at me from the closet, all signaled married to me.

When I wandered down the stairs and into the living room, where I'd left Lorne unpacking, I froze in the doorway. Each piece of furniture stood in a perfect straight line against the walls. Nothing at an angle, no chair set kitty-corner. Even the candles stood like marines along one shelf. I looked, horrified, from one row to the next. And the next and the next. Then I burst into tears. How had I landed in a perfectly aligned life when I had worked so hard to live anything but?

I grew up in a small, depressed mill town in Rhode Island, in the same house my great-grandparents bought when they emigrated from southern Italy in the late 1800s. My grandmother, Mama Rose, was born there, got married there, went on to have ten children in her childhood bedroom, and died sitting at the kitchen table after making enough sauce and meatballs to feed us for the next year. My mother—her ninth child—brother, and I moved in with Mama Rose while my father was based in Cuba for the navy in the early sixties. After he came home, he moved in, too. My father died fifteen years ago, but my mother still lives at 10 Fiume Street. The thought of leaving has never once crossed her mind. I, on the other hand, could only think about leaving that house, that town, the entire state.

Everyone in West Warwick followed the same predictable path. The town was made up of a cluster of small villages that had sprung up along the Pawtuxet River during the industrial revolution, and was dominated by churches and mills. Although the churches had official names—St. Anthony's, St. Joseph's, Sacred Heart—they were known as the Portuguese church, the French church, and the Italian church. The immigrants who came to work in those now-empty mills, lived in small neighborhoods together, and their ethnicity dominated those communities. The town's life cycle revolved around the various festivals held at these churches. The sight of *zeppole*, the cream-filled Italian pastries, in bakery windows signaled the beginning of spring. If the smell of *chourico* and the sounds of nonstop fireworks filled the air, we knew the Portuguese La-La had started and summer was over.

Catholic life ruled the town. Little girls in lace mantillas walked hand in hand to church with their black-clad grandmothers. Celebrations centered on church rituals: baptism, First Communion, confirmation. Every Sunday of my childhood I woke up to the sound of church bells. Not just the ones from Sacred Heart down the hill from us, but from all the churches all over town. In the school yard, we debated what to give up for Lent. We went to school late on Ash Wednesday, proudly showing off the smudge of ash on our foreheads. On February 2, we came to school late, stopping first at church to get our throats blessed, the long white taper candles passed solemnly under our chins as we knelt at the altar. If you felt really close to someone, you shared what you would tell the priest at confession on Saturday. Once, at recess, when we asked the new girl, Sandra Goldsmith, which church she went to, she burst into tears and confessed, "I'm not Catholic!" Then she ran home.

My father liked to say that our path was predetermined: we went from getting baptized at Sacred Heart, to having our wedding reception at the Club 400, to our wake at Prata's Funeral Home. Indeed, the Club 400 served up Italian wedding soup, ziti, and chicken Marsala to every bride and groom in town. In the center of the banquet room, a fountain bubbled out whiskey sours. On every table, paper plates sat heavy with cookies baked by grandmothers and aunts. The favors—a small tulle bundle of candy, tied by the bride's youngest siblings and cousins with a ribbon that matched the wedding theme color—never varied.

All of this sameness brought comfort and security to seemingly everyone in town. Except me. The day Sandra Goldsmith ran in shame from the playground, I felt jealous of her otherness. If she wasn't Catholic, then what was she? I imagined veiled women, minarets, mysterious chanting. At my cousin Cynthia's wedding at the Club 400, I vowed to have my own distant reception somewhere far away, like Newport or Providence. Or maybe I wouldn't get married at all, I thought as I watched the bridesmaids in cranberry velvet gowns clutching their colonial bouquets. Maybe our small-town path was set, but early on I was determined to veer from it as often and as far as possible. The first time I read Robert Frost's poem "The Road Less Traveled," I cried with relief. Here was my anthem, at last.

"Why are you crying?" Lorne asked me that morning, a look of complete bewilderment on his face.

I just shook my head and cried harder.

How could I put into words what I felt? How could I explain that this furniture that he had so carefully lined up against our living room and dining room walls represented a box, a failure, the road too traveled.

"Did I do something wrong?" he persisted.

"Everything is in a straight line!" I said.

Hearing the words out loud brought on a fresh round of sobs.

It is important to know that the person standing there crying was no young bride; I was thirty-eight years old. This was my second marriage, and I'd had my share of live-in boyfriends, brief intense relationships, and more than a few one-night stands. True to my long-ago vow to follow my own path, I had met this husband while I was separated but not divorced from the last husband. I had decided that I would never get married again, that once (for the record: in a meadow) was enough. Therefore, I hadn't bothered to get divorced. Within six months of meeting this husband, we decided to have a baby; two weeks later I was pregnant. On the morning I stood crying at the sight of that furniture, seeing it as a metaphor for my future, our one-and-a-half-year-old son, Sam, was upstairs asleep.

It would seem to anyone looking in, that despite the military decorating style, I had indeed fulfilled my desire to live an extraordinary
life. Despite everyone, from teachers to guidance counselors, telling
me that it was impossible to become a writer, I had found a way to do
just that. My path to my dream career was as kitty-corner as my path
to marriage and parenthood had been. In search of adventures, after
college I went to work as a TWA flight attendant instead of pursuing
an MFA in creative writing or taking an entry-level job at a magazine
or publishing house.

I fled West Warwick and the state of Rhode Island, moving to
Kansas City, Boston, St. Louis, and finally New York City. While
my friends shared Upper East Side apartments, I lived in a series of
studios in the East Village. Walking those streets alone, I felt my cells
rearrange themselves, settling into place for the first time. I ate cheap
Indian food on East Sixth Street and breakfast at old Polish diners.
My boyfriend was a handsome, sexy, mercurial actor. As we sat at
rooftop parties in our leather jackets drinking tequila and discussing
Mamet and Chekhov, or roamed the miles of books at the Strand
Book Store, I knew I was living the life I had imagined for myself. My
comfort came not from the familiar, but from the unknown. Nour-
ished on routine and ritual, I now woke every day not knowing what
lay ahead.

Eventually I married another writer, and my life spun into yet
more uncharted territories. The sound track to our life was the sound
of typewriter keys clacking. We moved to then-ungentrified Brooklyn,
writing our books in adjacent rooms, reading what we'd written out
loud to each other over dinner and wine each night. Most of our
friends were writers, too. I used to marvel that a girl from a mill town

had landed here, in New York City, surrounded by people who, like her, loved words.

Even when that marriage broke apart five years later, I did not change my kitty-corner ways. I moved to the way West Village with my two cats, and traveled to Egypt and beyond, collecting adventures and experiences, living a life that surpassed even my most outlandish girlhood fantasies. On the night I arrived at the University of Rhode Island to appear on an arts panel, I had no plans except to keep writing and keep living exactly as I pleased. When the handsome guy who kept appearing at my side all night literally blocked my way out and invited me for a drink, I said yes mostly because I said yes to just about everything.

Before we finished our first glass of wine, we had figured out that we had met over two decades ago on New Year's Eve at the Rhode Island premiere of the movie *The Poseidon Adventure*. Lorne had worked at camp with my high school boyfriend; he had grown up a mile from me; we had even overlapped at the same college for a couple of years. In other words, Lorne was everything I had run away from. Whereas many women would have seen danger in the other men in my life, Lorne's stability and steadiness terrified me. The next morning, I went back to New York, fast. But it was already too late.

This love, instead of hurtling me into an exciting future, sent me backward. Before long I was navigating familiar roads in a second-hand Volvo. The divorce I didn't think I needed was finalized. The place I wanted to leave was home again. Had I risked so much for so long only to land right back on the path I had so carefully avoided?

Even after I angled a chair in one corner and rearranged the pillar candles into a vague geometric shape; even after I hung all of my religious folk art on the walls and walked through the apartment smudging each room with a smoky sage stick; even after I tried to explain all of this to Lorne and he tried to understand, still I worried that I had made a huge mistake by moving back to Rhode Island.

When I went back to New York City that fall to teach a weekly class at NYU, I walked the maze of Village streets crying. Just as my cells had settled when I moved there, they now were all a jumble again. In Providence, I tried in vain to find a ballet class, a restaurant I loved, a supermarket that sold canned chipotles. No one looked like me or dressed like me or seemed to want the things I wanted. In fact, my life began to feel very much like the one I'd had as a young girl, the one where I was a misfit and longed to get away.

But it wasn't so easy this time. Here was a man I loved—loved! Here was a son I adored. Ten minutes away were my parents, delighted to have me back and grateful to live so close to their grandchild. Before I knew it, I had another baby, a daughter we named Grace. Before I knew it, my son was already in nursery school. Before I knew it, my father was diagnosed with terminal lung cancer. Now I was the grateful one, able to be at the hospital in a matter of minutes each time they called to tell me he had taken a turn for the worse. I knew these roads. Like kinesthetic memory, I drove them without having to think about anything except being at his side. For the last week of his life, I slept on a chair in his hospital room, knowing that my own little family waited just down the road.

In 2002, the unthinkable happened. My funny, smart five-year-old daughter, Grace, died suddenly from a virulent form of strep. Although in the days that followed, friends and family came from Oregon and California, North Carolina and Virginia, within hours, our home was full of friends and family who lived nearby. They arrived with pink flowers, single-malt whiskey, shoulders to cry on, and arms opened for hugs. They arrived, and they stayed until I could once again boil water to cook spaghetti, drive Sam to school, read a book.

In those terrible months after Grace died, I took comfort in the familiar: the sunlight on the tree outside my bedroom window, the sounds of my friends' voices, the safe refuge I found in my local coffee shop or at a friend's kitchen table. Routine and ritual got me through each day. I didn't answer the phone because I didn't know who waited at the other end. I stayed at home at night because my family's faces made me feel secure. I had spent my lifetime rejecting the very things and places that now buttressed me.

That first year of my marriage, I had trembled not in the face of routine, but in the face of change. I faltered at the challenge of finding my way when things lined up just right. I don't regret my resistance to a routine life. In that resistance I learned a lot about myself, about my own stubbornness and narrow-minded views about what mattered and how to achieve it. But of course I realize now that things are never lined up exactly as you hoped. Life keeps shifting no matter where you live or where you place your furniture. People break your heart. They die, no matter how fiercely you love them. But they hold your hand when you need it. They feed you. They walk beside you on both familiar and unfamiliar paths.

In this marriage I have stayed in for almost twenty years, I painted our walls royal blue, marigold orange, lavender. Our sofa is purple.

Our windows are lined with ropes of hot red peppers. But at night, on our well-worn sheets, the hand I hold as I drift off to sleep is one I know as well as my own. The last thing I hear is his breathing, predictable and soft. The last thing I smell is the faint scent of Irish Spring soap. The last thing I think, happily, is *Home*.

The First Fight

AMY WILSON

I may have been in a little bit of a bad mood, too. It was hard to ignore the slight sense of deflation. After throwing the best party we'd ever attended, with long-lost friends and tears and dancing till the hotel shut us down; after twelve days of lounging on a beach where drink-with-umbrella service started at noon; after the UPS guy stopped visiting each day, his dolly loaded with gifts, only the bills were left, plus a few piles of bubble-wrapped china we hadn't yet figured out where to store.

Still, we were newlyweds. We were supposed to be blissful and giggly. So why was David stomping around in the hallway, throwing down his attaché case with considerably more aggression than was necessary? We knew getting married wouldn't be a thunderclap of change—we'd already been living together in this very apartment for almost three years. We walked down the aisle calm and certain. While engaged, I had felt some smug superiority to those who wed barely knowing each other, who had never had a conversation about how many kids, or if kids, or what they wanted for the rest of their lives. I'd hear those women call in on talk radio, so disappointed and confused that their loved ones hadn't magically changed into different men after they were married. Somehow, to their wives' chagrin, these men had stubbornly remained the same assholes they always were. I thought those women were idiots, thinking marriage could solve everything. Or anything. But I was equally certain that we were different. In our case, marriage really was the solution: the very thing that would mean we never had to fight again, since all we ever fought about was whether we were going to get married.

"Are you mad about something?"

My husband (there it was, that word—still so awkward and formal) paused in his sorting of the day's mail on the kitchen counter. He closed his eyes, as if this question required far more patience than he had to give. As if he had to remain silent lest he scream something hateful. Not that he ever had—he was an almost maddening paragon of restraint. But I felt the silence was worse. It had been three days since he had initiated a conversation with me, three days since he had smiled or patted me on the rear while I was brushing my teeth. Three days since he had acted like he could even tolerate my company.

We had been here before; it happened a few times a year for as long as we had been together. The books all said that it was totally normal male behavior, and that when a man is In His Cave, the last thing a woman should do is stand in the mouth of that cave and yell inside, asking just when he's planning on coming out. The books said I should wait it out, not take it personally. Take a walk, call a girl-friend. And so I would, for three days, five days, a week, and then completely negate all that if-you-love-something-set-it-free claptrap by becoming angry and needy, self-righteous and desperate. I would become the very things most likely to drive him further underground.

"Are you even listening to me right now? Because you're not even acknowledging that I'm speaking. So, uh, it's kind of difficult for me to tell."

Sarcasm! That was sure to help. But I could never stop myself. Despite all David's after-the-fact assurances to the contrary, I was sure these sojourns inward were about me, a weighing of whether he was committed to me for the long haul. He was testing what life without me might be like by acting as if that's where he already lived. And it seemed to be so easy for him to shut me out, even if I was right there in the room with him, puffed up with hurt feelings and pretty hard to miss. The books all said that if I could just patiently wait out these times in my man's life, our relationship would be the better for it, since my man would eventually reemerge more firmly committed than ever. Maybe they were right; I wouldn't know, since I was never able to be that patient.

Of course, some would say I had been plenty patient, since we were together for three and a half years before we got engaged, four and a half before we were married. My boyfriend (like most men) could be totally psyched about his sister getting engaged, and his roommate, then his other roommate, without noticing that they had all started dating their intendeds well after we had. We got some good-natured teasing about this from family and friends, but deep down I was sure they didn't think it was funny. I was sure they were all looking at me for the reason he still hadn't proposed. It had to be my shortcoming that was keeping us on the sidelines, keeping me single at the blasphemous age of almost-thirty. David, on the other hand, didn't see what the hurry was, and all my tears and upset did not exactly hasten his yearning to yoke his future to mine. As long as I didn't focus on when—or whether—we would have a wedding, we had an easy, happy relationship. But when David went into his cave, sooner or later I would panic. And we would fight.

"Can you not even look at me? Jesus Christ, what is the matter with you?"

But none of that was going to matter now. My husband wouldn't need to withdraw! Our public commitment would ipso facto render any waffling moot. We were married; we were never going to have this fight again. We had walked down that aisle free of second thoughts or cares, so excited, so ready to be married at last.

Yet three weeks after the wedding, here we were.

"You promised you wouldn't push me away! You promised! How can you do this to me? I'm your *wife*!"

David really had promised not to do this anymore, because he hated how upset it made me, he didn't want that—and what guy wants another where-is-this-relationship-going all-nighter, anyhow? But after thirteen days out of the office, the pressure at his already extremely stressful job was no doubt considerable. He had also recently considered switching jobs and, throughout our honeymoon, fielded increasingly frantic calls from the human resources departments on both sides of that decision. (In the end, he decided to stay where he was.) It was probably all of this, not second thoughts about having married me, that was consuming him. If I had had a day like that, I would come home, flop next to him on the couch, turn off the TV so that I might have his undivided attention, and then keep up a one-sided conversation until bedtime. I could not conceive that he might do things differently.

"Will you just say something? Anything?"

Still leaning against the kitchen counter, David stayed silent. He probably figured that any protest he made that it wasn't about me would only bring a smackdown accusation that he was lying right to my face. But if he was intent on not fighting with me, I was equally intent on flushing him out into the open, on saying whatever I needed to say to make him mad enough to yell back.

"I can't live like this. I'm not kidding! If this is how things are going to be, I want a divorce!"

I didn't mean it, of course. I was trying to make a dent in his armor. Being ridiculous on purpose, lobbing a grenade no one could ignore. There it lay between us. I saw David's eyes widen, but only for a half moment—then he lowered them again, that practiced look of indifference that so infuriated me. He said nothing. Now I really was scared.

"Is that what YOU want?"

He wouldn't answer. Even though I was the one who had brought it up, I was sickened with the sudden certainty that I had hit it on the head. I could see it all laid out before me: returning the presents. Telling our family members, who would be shocked. Shocked! What could possibly have changed in three weeks? And it would all be my fault (even if it was David who wanted it) because I was the one who had said the word in a moment of melodrama, a carelessly powerful word that felt like it couldn't not take shape now that it had been uttered.

Before a couple is married, ultimatums can be bandied about in rocky times: "Maybe I should move out," or "I just need some space." And while they're upsetting to hear, they are also, on some level, permitted. It is discourse within the bounds of reason for a couple who has not yet made a solemn lifetime commitment in front of all their relatives and loved ones. Standing there in the kitchen, I saw that this was different: Now we were either in or out. The time for equivocation was over. Saying the word *divorce* carried such a weight of finality and pain that I felt it must have damaged our newborn marriage even to have said it out loud. "Divorce" was not something one said unless one meant it. I understood that. Now that it was too late.

I had expected David to play his part, say that was ridiculous, there I went again. Now neither of us knew what to say. I turned and walked out of the room, gingerly, lest I say or do something that would make things even worse. We retreated to opposite corners of our not-very-big apartment for the rest of the evening, neither one of us sure what had happened, what the other person thought, what would happen next.

By the time I got into bed, I was shaking.

"I don't want—what I said—to happen," I whispered to my husband's turned back, trying not to cry.

For a few moments, nothing.

"I don't either," David murmured, already mostly asleep.

I lay awake for a while, trying to remember just what it was that had been worth fighting about.

We were extra polite to each other for a while after that, the memory of the word lingering in the air long after it seemed politic to mention it. Some couples can fight and say things they don't mean and then laugh about it, years later—or even days. Just a funny story to tell at parties. "Paul! Remember when you burned the Thanksgiving turkey and I threw it right at your head? You should have seen yourself duck!" But I live with a certainty that the hurtful things said and done to me are the most truly and deeply meant. I think my husband is the same way. Our hurt feelings do not have a sense of humor. We need to be more careful.

And we are. We have never fought like that again. Perhaps it was only after that fight that we really were married, with a new and tacit understanding that our lives together might go further if we *did* take our relationship for granted, if we never argued the fact of its existence no matter how angry we were. Marriage might not have changed my husband's moodiness, but it could change my insecurity about it. His occasional trip to Eeyore's Gloomy Place wasn't about him deciding whether he wanted to be with me or not. It was just something he did—and something I had known well about when I pledged to spend my life with him. Being married means accepting that your life partner can be in a really shitty mood every once in a while and it might have absolutely nothing to do with you. Except when it's exactly totally about you. And that's okay, too.

The books were right, by the way. Thirteen years later, I can't even remember the last time David went on caveman retreat. I know it still happens, but these days when I can tell my husband is in a bad mood, I stay out of his way. Let him catnap in front of *SportsCenter.* Wait for him to feel like talking, and sooner or later, he does. Maybe my not needling him actually helps him come back to me more quickly; maybe he's just learned to brood more efficiently over the years. But things are easier now. There is a security, a safety, a filing of the edges that comes with marriage—just not with three weeks of marriage. We hadn't earned it yet.

Today our marriage feels safe as sweatpants, blessed in its calmness. But when we hear about people getting divorced, whether friends or friends' parents or people we met once seven years ago, we lie in bed and wonder how it happened. We are human, of course: we always search for that one difference, a forgotten unlocked side door, that proves we can still consider ourselves safe from such intrusion in our own lives. I have never totally lost the fear of divorce, the sudden understanding I had the night of our first fight. There is something about divorce that can come in unbidden through the keyhole, taking away the one you love right in front of you, a little bit at a time. It's the leaver who sees it coming; afterward, it seems, the left swear they never had the slightest warning. By the time one smells the gas, it is already too late.

Marriage is two people promising to keep that danger from the doorstep together, or at least to say they see it coming, even when (especially when) their loved one doesn't. It's a balance between knowing when to give your loved one a break, or space, or time, and knowing when you really do need to speak up. That part is something we are still figuring out. But after thirteen years, our worst trials would seem risible to some, and even though we have never taken the bubble wrap off our wedding china, life without each other has become unthinkable. That means we are very lucky. Maybe that first fight needed to be fought—but it was also, in some ways, our last.

Love in the Time of Camouflage

MARGARET DILLOWAY

One evening, not long after we were married, my husband did not come home from work.

I waited. Dinner grew cold. No phone calls came in. I grew anxious. Was he lying by the side of the freeway someplace? Had he been called away? Or was he simply inconsiderate? I had no idea.

I was alone in Tacoma, Washington. My family and friends were down in San Diego.

The day after my husband and I met, which was New Year's Eve, 1996, standing on a wall in Las Vegas, drinking cheap beer out of plastic token cups, he told me he wanted to marry me. I thought he was nutty. I'd just gotten out of an ill-advised young marriage, I was twenty-two years old, and I had plans.

We spent a few months apart, writing letters, calling, visiting when possible. I loved his single-minded devotion to me, his long letters filled with cartoons, poetry, and odd short stories. If the world ended, he'd be the one I'd want around. I decided to ignore just about every Dear Abby advice column I'd ever read. Keith had only enlisted for a total of three years, and perhaps had only two more to go, but it seemed too long. I moved to Washington and we married in October 1997, in a ceremony only our parents knew about.

Finally, three hours later, Keith arrived home, still in his camouflage military uniform. His battle-dress uniform, or BDU, daily wear, they called it; starched so stiff it could almost stand alone. "Where were you?" I asked.

"Being punished," my husband said, taking off his black Ranger beret. "My platoon sergeant said you made his wife cry."

I was confused. I'd never met the sergeant's wife. I hadn't met any of the wives except for the few in my husband's immediate small group, or squad. "I did not."

"Apparently you yelled at her." My husband smiled wryly. "The sergeant said, 'Dilloway, I had to listen to my wife crying about your wife, so now I'm going to punish you.'"

Oh. I swallowed a hard lump, trying to read Keith, figure out if he was mad at me. I'd probably be furious at him if our positions were reversed.

The wife in question was the family support coordinator, the one who organized the activities designed to provide support to the Ranger families. She had not invited us to the family picnic. I had found out about the picnic after it happened, during some wives' meeting where everyone talked about it. It felt like being the only kid in the class not invited to a birthday party.

So I called her and asked her to please let me know about events in the future, because I would like to go. I may have added that though I understood it was unintentional, if I had her job, I'd remember how lonely it was to be new, try to include everyone. I didn't yell.

I explained this to him as he unlaced his boots.

"I'm sorry," I finished, finally, thoroughly confused. "I don't know what I said."

He enveloped me in a hug, crushing me deliciously against him. Two-hour daily workouts and twenty-mile road marches with heavy packs will do that. "It's not your fault," he said.

I blinked away tears. I didn't know anyone in the unit. My husband's immediate squad-team members were mostly unmarried, so I only saw other wives during larger general meetings. If I were the family coordinator, I would want to know who needed support and welcome them.

It wasn't that simple.

This was my first clue that married life with an Army Ranger was going to be very different from being married to a civilian.

I'd never intended to marry someone in the military. Military wives must be strong and independent, and while superficially I appeared to be so, in fact I was a morass of deep neediness (see: early marriage). Keith, my husband, had decided to join for the adventure and for the experience; he wanted to be in the FBI or U.S. marshals. He had a bachelor's in classics and was working at a going-nowhere desk job when he enlisted. Except, on his way to airborne training, he met me.

Actually, we'd first met when I was fourteen and he was eighteen. Keith was a friend of my brother's. My brother had knocked on my bedroom door one morning, opened it, and said, "Hey, this is my little sister. This is Keith." I have little recollection of this meeting. I remembered him for calling my pet cat "Big Cat" and that my mother liked him. Keith remembers me as a little kid wearing thick glasses.

And now here I was, learning that, indeed, military life was different from civilian life, and there was something like a secret rule book being passed around. Not only was there a defined hierarchy, there was an unwritten one, too.

Keith was in the 2nd Battalion of the 75th Ranger Regiment, a part of special operations, which includes, among others, the Green Berets and Navy SEALs. Army Rangers are a light and quick force, an all-male commando unit that jumps out of airplanes. They're the ones who went up Point du Hoc on D-Day; liberated Grenada; they were the subject of the book *Black Hawk Down.* Their unit compound is walled in, topped with barbed wire, and signage that says *Use of Lethal Force Authorized.* Which means they're allowed to shoot if you look suspicious.

The Rangers themselves had, it was rumored, the same general psychological profiles as serial killers. Hair-trigger tempers were encouraged. These men tended to settle personal disputes by hand, fighting in a sawdust fight pit, where the Gracie brothers had taught submission holds. When another soldier called a painting I'd made crappy, my husband told him they could settle the question in the "pit." The other Ranger refused.

Disputes between Rangers and non-Rangers, however, aroused the wrath of the entire Ranger Battalion, much like an older brother rising up to protect his little brother. Once, a Ranger dating a female soldier from another unit had gotten beat up by a group of men when he went to pick her up; his unit returned to the barracks in the middle of the night, locked the exits, and pummeled the entire group. No one reported it.

The main goal for a newbie like my husband was to go to Ranger school, a three-month-long course at Fort Benning, Georgia. Once you went through this, then you didn't have to be punished by doing things like clipping the grass with nail scissors. You would be promoted. Until then, you were treated sort of like a newbie at an especially unruly fraternity—except for the whole deadly weapons part.

Shortly after the wife incident, the entire battalion went away for a month to train. While everyone's spouses were gone, I tried to figure out where I fit in with the wives. Some rules were easy to comprehend. There are, of course, ranks in the military. Officers hold four-year college degrees and get saluted. Everyone else is enlisted. My husband, despite his college degree, had enlisted as a specialist, which meant that his pay almost qualified for food stamps, except that he got extra called "jump pay" for his jumping out of airplanes, pushing us just over the salary limit.

During our first year, Keith was away three-quarters of the time—my husband went to Panama, Germany, the East Coast, California, Nevada, and various other undisclosed locations for training. Though this was pre-9/11, when no one flew American flags and everyone believed we were safe, the Rangers were always ready to go at a moment's notice. Sometimes my husband could not be more than an hour away from returning to base, in case he had to be deployed.

His job was a forward observer, someone who sneaks ahead and radios airplanes to tell them where to drop bombs. He came in first on the forward-observer tests, and was optimistic about his chances to go to Ranger school.

Meanwhile, I'd just graduated from a liberal arts college in Claremont, an ivory tower of political correctness. As I was trying to navigate this new Darwinian world, I got a temporary job at a place that produced two weekly newspapers, one a city paper for Tacoma and one for the army. I did bulk mailings and entered classified ads. I intercepted a fax asking for reporters to fly on a C-141B; timidly, I asked the editor if I could go, and he said yes. I took Dramamine and was the only reporter who didn't throw up. Before long, I was free-lancing on the side.

A few months after we married, our names came up on the base housing waiting list. We moved into a brick town house across the street from an airfield, planes landing early in the morning with thundering din. These would be condemned shortly after we moved out, with the white linoleum of schoolhouses for the living room floors.

All the lower-enlisted families lived together, from all sorts of jobs. In the middle of the night, I awakened to the sounds of the soldier next door shouting at his wife. "You don't know how much stress I'm under! My job is hard!" the husband yelled once. He was a file clerk who worked in an office between 9 a.m. and 4 p.m., with a ninety-minute lunch every day. The day started at five or earlier for my husband, and went on until after six in the evening or into the night. Other times, he was called into work at night, and wouldn't return for days.

Though I now lived among soldiers' families, it was still hard to make friends. We were different. When my husband, in the black Ranger beret that was then exclusive to them, walked across the yard to his car, the neighbors stopped what they were doing and watched. If he waved, they waved back. If he didn't wave, no one spoke.

One morning, I looked out into the common backyard to see two four-year-olds engaged in a full-on fistfight, the mothers watching. I banged open the screen door. "What's going on?" I asked as calmly as I could.

"They were arguing," one mother answered, "so we decided to let them fight it out." Both of them were perhaps twenty, maybe younger. "Do you think we shouldn't?" Her question was genuinely earnest, her brow wrinkling as she waited for my answer.

I blinked at them, wondering if I'd landed on another planet. "Probably not." Later, I found it wasn't unusual around here to judge force as the best way to own another human being. At a picnic, a first sergeant's son ran around punching the Rangers who ranked lower than his father in the testicles as his father watched with amusement; the men couldn't say anything to their superior.

I worried Keith would change, turn into someone worse than that clerk next door; or that maybe he was the type of person who thrived on violence, and I simply didn't know it yet. Whenever he was home, it was like a strange honeymoon, each of us careful to spend as much time as possible with each other, figure out our boundaries. I always dropped whatever I had managed to get going on to spend this time with him.

When he could, he went to plays with me, local productions. I went to everything in the area: high school productions, community college productions, community plays. Inevitably, in the dark, tired from spending multiple days awake, he would fall asleep. I'd only poke him if he snored.

One morning, he asked if I wanted eggs. He made me an omelet, a thing so large it wouldn't fit on the plate. "How many eggs did you use?" I asked.

"Thirteen," he said. "Why?" He finished off what I couldn't.

At Thanksgiving, he brought home his buddy—one of the soldiers he'd just been away with for three weeks. Without telling me. The guy in question wasn't the problem; he was a gangly eighteen-year-old, far away from home; it was that Keith brought him back without asking.

"Don't you want to spend time with me?" I asked. "I missed you."

"Of course I do," he said. "I should have called. But he doesn't have anywhere to go for Thanksgiving. Don't worry. I'll cook."

I couldn't negate my husband's kind heart. As we progressed through the weekend, the young man chuckling at Keith's raw turkey, sleeping on the couch, playing us at video games, I had an epiphany. There was another entity in this relationship. Not this young man specifically, but the army. A mistress who would always come first. I was the second wife to his primary wife, only having custody of him on off days. And on those off days, the men he worked with would almost always be included. By necessity; these were the men he depended on to save his life. And I had better treat them like brothers.

At work, a full-time writing position opened. I got to do things civilians never do. Once, the Rangers had a family Range Day. We went out to a firing range, where I hunkered down with a machine gun and a rifle. The hot shells hit my side, and I'm scared of guns, but I didn't dare flinch.

It wasn't long before I figured out if I was going to write anything critical, it had better be under a pen name. Every time there was an article vaguely critical of the army, even if I didn't write it, Keith would get flack. I mostly wrote happy articles about the military. One of the new columns featured an inspiring military family member. I looked for Ranger wives doing interesting things. Once I picked a first sergeant's wife, who earned extra income helping a shut-in. Her house was cinder blocks on the outside, but on the inside it was a homey woman's domain that could pack up and move at a moment's notice. She had a nearly wall-to-wall fluffy pink carpet she took on each move. "My husband knows this is my space," she said proudly, her husband being a notoriously difficult guy, with his name tattooed across his knuckles. After his wife was featured in the newspaper, the first sergeant was, grudgingly, nicer to my husband. The wives became, if not friendly, polite to me. They invited me to picnics and the Christmas party.

I, in turn, never got over my abject terror that somehow I'd say the wrong thing and my husband would be spit-polishing someone's shoes for six months. The officers' wives did not hang out with the enlisted wives; that would be even more fearsome. I still kept to myself. I learned how to be polite, not complain.

And, for the first time, I learned I could get along alone. The independence required for a military life, it seemed, could be acquired. "I love it when my husband's gone," one woman confided to me. "I let the house go and I can do whatever I want."

Finally, my husband's turn came up for Ranger school. He did the tests—push-ups, pull-ups, a run—and passed. He came home happy, ready to pack. Then, when he returned to work, he got this news. "You didn't do all the pull-ups," a sergeant told him abruptly. His squad sergeant was away training, and wasn't there to speak up for him. "You're not going."

That was that. Keith's goal of going to Ranger school was over. Now, with a little over a year left in the unit, they transferred him to the headquarters unit, as close to an office job as you could get in his unit. The Ranger school slot went to someone who had reenlisted. Keith went on fewer training missions; he rode his bike to work, came home early most days. Just as I'd gotten used to the crazy schedule, it turned into a normal one.

But though both our dreams and goals had changed that first year, sometimes disappointingly, we learned we could depend on each other, no matter what. And, in a strange twist, it was only by becoming an army dependent that I had finally become independent, someone who wasn't afraid of loneliness. In marriage, I discovered my own small brand of toughness.

525,600 *Minutes*

JENNA McCARTHY

Many people believe that the first year of marriage is one of the hardest, a transitional period of extreme sacrifice, compromise, and adjustment. I am not one of these people. In fact, I am pretty sure that if you find the opening twelve months as newlyweds to be tough, you are in for a long and rocky road to side-by-side cemetery plots.

I say this based on the assumption that you married someone whom you knew for some length of time greater than a few hours or days. (Mail-order brides and Carmen Electra can skip to the next essay; there's really nothing for you here.) You asked him what he did for a living and what that job entailed, saw him eat, and negotiated your divergent tastes in movies and music. You probably rode in some type of vehicle simultaneously at least once. You met each other's family and decided to stay together anyway. Eventually he got on bended knee or rented a banner plane and gave you a ring that he (actually, now, the collective you) still will be making monthly installments on five years from now. You knew with an absolute confidence that allowed you to profess your everlasting love and devotion in front of God and family that he was your soul mate, the one and only. You planned the mother of all parties together—well, he watched you do it and maybe went to the cake-tasting thingy—and afterward spent a week attempting complicated new sexual positions on a balcony in Aruba. Then you came back to your lovely marital home, the one overflowing with fluffy matching towels and a fortune in All-Clad pots and pans and enough gift cards to tile your master bathroom, and discovered that the son of a bitch you just wed eats sunflower seeds in bed and couldn't close his underwear drawer that last half an inch if someone held a gun to his testicles.

What the fuck? Where are the romantic candlelit dinners and the sunset strolls wearing matching white outfits like they promised you in the marriage brochures? Where's the chocolate Lab puppy and the white picket fence and the doting, happy husband wearing his "My Grill's Hotter Than Yours" apron, flipping filets for you and your closest couple friends? Where are the roses, the spontaneous tokens of affection, the philosophical debates over the meaning of existence that you can only have with your life partner? And how could he forget that today is your five-and-a-half-month anniversary?

If you were expecting marriage to be a nonstop parade of rainbows and back rubs that don't double as foreplay, I guess I can understand the whole miserable-first-year bit. Otherwise, consider a few realities: in the lifetime of togetherness you just signed up for, these 525,600 minutes are pretty much your extended honeymoon. Odds are he's still occasionally opening your car door for you, grabbing your ass (in a flirty and not annoying way), and actually listening when you talk. You probably don't have thirteen kids to fight about, you haven't gained forty-five pounds apiece, and while his boisterous snoring may no longer fall into the "adorable" category, it also doesn't make you want to smother him yet. You have time and energy for things like date nights and sex. It will be years before one of you will storm into the bathroom uninvited and attempt to have a conversation without actually noticing or caring that the other is on the toilet. Peer, if you will, into my imaginary crystal ball:

Future Him [throwing open the bathroom door with a startling flourish]: "Honey, do you know where I left my tape measure?"

Future You [not even bothering to put down your *People* magazine]: "I'm a little busy at the moment."

Future Him [exasperated]: "I'm not asking you to *get* it; I just want to know if you know where it is."

Future You [scrutinizing Demi Moore's impossibly line-free face and wondering exactly how much work she's had done]: "Would you mind giving me just a minute? I'm on the toilet here, in case you didn't notice."

Future Him: "Who cares?"

Future You: "I do."

Future Him: "You should light a match."

Future You: *"GET OUT OF THIS BATHROOM, YOU FUCKING ASSHOLE!"*

Relative to the rest of your married life, there will be few times in those initial fifty-two weeks of wedlock when you will call your husband a fucking asshole. For one thing, you'll still be comparatively high on the drugs known as hormones that propel two people in love to commit to a lifetime of togetherness in the first place and then temporarily blind them to the host of behaviors that will one day drive them both batshit crazy. Secondly, you will be extremely busy writing thank-you notes and finding ways to throw the words *my husband* into every third sentence. In your remaining slivers of free time, you will be folding his boxer briefs or marveling at the way the sunlight glints off the eternity band on your left hand or searching for new and exciting Crock-Pot recipes. (He'll be watching TV.) And in most cases, it takes more than a dozen months for the deep-seated anger and resentment born of proximity to fester to "fucking asshole" levels.

I'm not saying you won't experience a few newlywed hiccups. After all, depending on whether or not you were among the 70 percent of couples who live together in sin prior to tying the knot, there may be some logistics to work out: Who will pay the bills? Will you have two separate bank accounts or one joint one? Who will do the grocery shopping, the laundry, the cooking, the yard work, the bill paying, the taxes? Who gets to decide where you go on your vacations or whether you buy the new couch that you want or the pool table that he wants? Whose family will you spend holidays with? Who gets to park in the single garage spot? Will you load the dishwasher using his random and haphazard method or your clearly superior painstaking approach? If you both want to watch different shows on TV at the same time, how do you choose? Which way should the toilet paper come off the roll? (This one's a no-brainer because most men are incapable of replacing an empty tube anyway.)

While this early period in your union might involve some degree of compromise and negotiation, your disputes should be reasonably minor in both scope and importance. If your marriage were a dog, all of the first-year "adjustment issues" combined would be a single, tiny fleabite compared to the crippling arthritis, festering scabies, and rotting teeth typical of older marriages. Hopefully neither of you is considering having—or actually *is* having—an affair. You're not yet arguing about whether his public school education is good enough for your children or if they deserve the same swanky private experience you had, or which of your crazy relatives would assume custody of your spawn should God forbid something happen to you both. You're not freaking out because you haven't saved enough money for a new toaster, no less retirement. Your health is damn near as good as it's going to get. In other words, you're not thinking about all of those hypothetical extremes—illness, poverty, abject misery—you vowed wouldn't put the slightest damper on your eternal devotion.

Think back to your very first real job. I don't care if you're flipping burgers or flying jumbo jets; every field has entry-level underlings with entry-level responsibilities. My first gig was as an assistant in the traffic department of a large advertising agency, which essentially meant that I carried stacks of papers around all day and waited for important people to sign them. The task was simple (get the papers signed), the expectations clear (they must have signatures), and I possessed the necessary skills to complete it (legs to carry me from one important person to the next and eyes that could detect signatures). Plus, unlike many of my recently graduated friends, I had a job. Who cares if it was mindlessly, miserably boring? I got to wear cute clothes and use the park-and-ride shuttle, so I felt like a grown-up. Other than having my wallet stolen out of my office once and suffering an unseemly crush on one of my coworkers, it was pretty drama-free.

Somehow I managed to pick up a few skills at this job, and assumed some greater responsibilities; once I got to sign some papers *myself*. I started climbing the ladder. With each rung my title became more impressive, my office a little swankier, my salary a smidge bigger. I began writing my own ads for smaller clients, then the larger ones. Eventually I was creating entire campaigns from concept through completion. There was much more stress, of course—now I had not just my boss and her boss breathing down my neck, but clients of my own depending on me not to screw up. Yet even with the added pressure, I wouldn't have traded places with my lowly, bored replacement traffic assistant for all of the stirrup pants in the world. (What? This was the early 1990s.) I won a few awards and had confidence and the respect of my coworkers. I wasn't the boss yet, but I also wasn't scared of her. Once I called her a fucking asshole to her face. She laughed, and I knew I had job security.

Honestly, being married is a lot like that. When your hunky new husband carries you over that threshold, you're not expected to know or do very much. (Mostly show up, shut up, and put out.) The responsibilities and their subsequent challenges are added slowly, layer by layer. You buy a house, then maybe a bigger one. Your jobs get more demanding, which seems like a fine time to pop out a few kids. One of you gets sick (hopefully nothing serious), you take a couple of vacations, maybe attempt a home-improvement project or thirty. Someone loses a job or a parent, or gets really depressed or buys a sports car or considers a face-lift. Your friends start having affairs and getting divorced and your retirement account is a few zeros short of the comfort zone. I hate to sound harsh, but if you're that daunted by the raging toilet-paper debate or his inability to launch his dirty socks all the way into the hamper instead of in the general vicinity of it, either your expectations were a tad lofty going in or maybe—just maybe— you married the wrong person. (It happens. Look at Renée Zellweger, Janet Jackson, and Drew Barrymore.)

Marriage as a whole isn't easy, to some extent because monogamy isn't our biological destiny and also because of the living-together- forever part. Happily ever after? A myth. Anyone who tells you otherwise is lying or delusional. You'll disagree, bicker, and maybe even one day throw a shoe or a lamp or a plate of spaghetti at your husband. You will lie to him ("Botox? What Botox?") or catch him lying to you ("Strip club? What strip club?") on at least one occasion. When he storms away from you in the middle of a fight, you will give him the finger behind his back because you can't scream what you really want to with the kids right there listening. You'll complain about him to your friends so often and so loudly that even you will get sick of hearing it. When your sweet, innocent children are safely out of earshot, you will call him a *fucking asshole* and mean it with every fiber of your being. I'm not condoning or endorsing any of this, mind you; I'm just saying it will happen. Hopefully by the time it does, you will have built a life together on a foundation so rock solid that you'll both still be standing—together, and maybe even smiling—when the dust settles.

Some people exercise because they thoroughly enjoy the grueling pain of working out; the rest of us do it for the results. Marriage is no different. As challenging as it is to commit your life to another human being, the payoffs are profound: Folks who forsake all others are happier, healthier, live longer, and have more money and sex than our swinging single friends. We get to have someone by our side in sickness and in health, for better or for worse. We have a mostly unbiased adult in the house we can ask, "Do these pants make my butt look big?" and who will capture and kill the very large spider over our bed. If we are so inclined, we can combine our DNA to create brand-new people, practically from scratch, and then we have someone who will watch those people for free when we go to Palm Springs with our girlfriends. If we're extraordinarily lucky, we'll still be bitching and bickering when we are so old that we don't care which way the toilet paper rolls because we can't wipe our own asses anyway.

WE WILL SURVIVE

Shared Anniversary

DAPHNE UVILLER

With apologies to my children, I can confidently say that my wedding day was the happiest day of my life, a goal I mocked when wedding vendors used it to try to win our business.

"I know you want this to be the most special, the most perfect day—"

"No." I would interrupt the well-meaning catering contestant. "If this is the most perfect day, does that mean it's all downhill after this?"

Before she began her confused apologies, I soothed her: "It doesn't have to be perfect. I just need to wind up married to Sacha."

But in fact, it was a glorious, scorching day on the banks of the Hudson River (nine years before Chelsea Clinton had the same idea). Except for one friend, our cohort was still childless and thus full of energy, enthusiasm, spontaneity. My dad was alive and healthy. My mother, with authority vested in her by the state of New York, married us with unsurpassed art and wisdom. We danced our butts off. And, icing on the cake, a friend confided that her chronically ill mother was up for a heart transplant that could put an end to her troubles and give her another thirty years on this earth. We all still moved about in a bubble of innocence we became aware of only after it popped.

No one who was there forgets our anniversary. It turned out to be a good-bye party to the way the world was.

. . . .

Less than forty-eight hours later, we were atop a ridge in the Shawan-gunk Mountains when a pair of tourists told us two planes had hit the World Trade Center. I actually didn't believe them, took them for a pair of morons. A few hours later, when we finally got through to New York City, a remote reality began to dawn as my father reassured me that my mother was alive and walking uptown from her office. Another friend left a message that he'd begun a phone chain to account for our wedding guests, many of whom were scheduled to be on flights home to California or Boston that morning. That was day two of our marriage.

. . . .

On September 12, we were supposed to head home to start the rest of our lives, but all of Manhattan was in lockdown. Instead, we drove to my in-laws, who lived upstate, not far from our honeymoon hotel. During breaks from the news, we opened the wedding presents we'd had shipped there instead of to our small apartment. I've tried to understand how I was able to take some pleasure in excavating new wine-glasses and linen place mats and even a melon baller from the folds of

Crate & Barrel tissue paper. I'd glance up at the screen, watch my native city burn, then snip open another box. Denial? Shock? A desire for tangible evidence that our married life was beginning—gleaming, unchipped, unstained—regardless of what the world threw at us?

Two of Sacha's relatives were also staying at his parents' house, stranded after the wedding, unable to get flights home to points west. One of them was so anxious she could barely speak to us; she'd worked up the courage to leave an ailing husband in order to attend our celebration, only to be punished for her generosity. She spent most of her time on the phone making sure he had enough to eat, that he was warm enough, that he hadn't fallen. At one point she answered call waiting and handed the phone to Sacha. He listened to the new call, his face calm. It was only from the pauses that I sensed something—else—wrong.

He hung up and took me aside, his eyes bright. We'd been waiting for the other shoe to drop, to learn that someone we knew had been in the towers or unlucky enough to have been downtown.

"Alice died last night."

Alice was not someone who was downtown. Alice was the mother of our friend, the friend who'd reported that we might be looking at a new chapter for her mother. It was a coda of a fuck-you from the universe: hey, what's one more life today?

We didn't open any more presents after that. Two planes into two buildings had been surreal enough to permit a kind of compartmentalization. This grief was a knee to the chest, utterly perceivable, and would have shaded our honeymoon in any context. We held each other and wept.

That was day three of our marriage.

. . . .

On day four, a national guardsman rested one hand on a police barricade and the other on his rifle and regarded the dried-up bouquet I shook at him. His face revealed nothing. He wasn't going anywhere. His job that day was to start with no, and then let people prove their cases, like a script reader in Hollywood. The line behind my husband-of-ninety-six hours and me was growing longer, literally by the second. I started to dig through our suitcase. I began to babble.

"I swear to you, he's been living here for months. But he was finishing grad school and moving in and planning the wedding, and also, we went to Hawaii before the wedding because he had this conference there, so he hasn't had time to change his license. That's why this was a short honeymoon. We were even supposed to be back yesterday, but we couldn't get home. We couldn't get home."

With all the tragedy flaming around us after the planes hit the towers, this was the part that, selfishly, upset me the most at that moment. I count my blessings every day, and one of them is a variation on "I'm grateful I don't live in a country where tanks roll down Fifth Avenue." For the first time in my privileged life, I was getting a taste of freedom curtailed: we were required to show identification to reach our West Thirteenth Street apartment, which was still cordoned off as part of the dead zone. I had lived in that building since I was eight years old, but Sacha didn't have a shred of evidence to prove that this was now his one and only home.

"Here!" I shouted. "Look." I waved a newspaper clipping at him with the hand not clutching dead flowers. "Our wedding announcement. See?"

The phlegmatic officer either took pity on me or got tired of our holding up the line. He stepped back and let us squeeze through the splintery blue barricade. It wasn't the threshold I'd imagined crossing.

. . . .

In theory, the first year of a modern marriage between offspring of liberal-minded families shouldn't be much more than a ceremonial transition, an uneventful twelve months preceded by cohabitation and followed sometime later by births, illnesses, and deaths. Compared to those rocky events, why should the procurement of a piece of paper with a seal on it shift the ground beneath you? How could signing a license be as momentous as the day Sacha moved in, a day that a man untroubled by accumulation threw his lot in with a sworn purger? And certainly, uttering vows under a pretty white tent wasn't more upending than what has followed: children born, parents getting sick, parents dying, mortgages (both approved and denied), renovations, uprootedness, often all together at the same time.

Why, even, should the officialization have been more momentous than the engagement, the moment at which we truly committed to spending our lives together? The wedding was just the party celebrating the decision we'd already made.

And yet.

Think about marriages that end, or begin to end, before the first anniversary. There has to be something about the vow taking that sheds light on problems that couldn't be seen or articulated before the ceremony (not unlike hitting send on a sensitive e-mail; the action suddenly highlights every flaw you couldn't see before). Certainly, many of us have teetered on the edge of marrying the wrong person. Years ago, when a six-year relationship of mine ended, my mother, though comforting and sympathetic, expressed relief that we didn't have to get married to get divorced. I don't tend to give much blanket advice, but this I know is true: if you get to a point where you say, "We need to either marry or break up," then please, please do everyone a favor and break up. A marriage should be a progression forward, not the result of a coin toss at a T-stop that led you left instead of right.

. . . .

Those who follow the coin-toss route probably suffer from a larger problem of false expectations: whatever's wrong with the relationship will be fixed by the Magic of Marriage, a sweet but misguided hope that there's a powerful tool available for purchase upon the tossing of the bouquet. These people must believe that getting married is like gaining entry to a secret club that will reveal heretofore unobtainable knowledge. They discover during the first year that this is not the case.

And under the harsh light of tragedy—death, illness, terrorist attack—perhaps that discovery is made during the first month. For better or worse, misfortune throws into sharp relief the contours of a nascent marriage. So if one member of the couple has to leave the country immediately following the wedding, it's a little tough to gauge how the marriage is doing in the face of said misfortune.

. . . .

Three weeks after our wedding, Sacha, a professional entomologist, began a two-month stint in the Bolivian jungle capturing dung beetles. As a grad student, he'd traveled to Bolivia many times during our courtship and I was familiar with the totality of his absence: no Internet access, no phone calls. He would land in Santa Cruz, load up on eight weeks' worth of rice for him and his fieldhands, find a working car, and take a perilous, bumpy, dusty two-day drive away from civilization, during which the car was sure to break down at least twice. (Doing science in developing countries requires an aptitude for auto mechanics.) To communicate with him, I e-mailed his coworker's wife, who then drove to a museum in Santa Cruz once a week to radio our husbands. She'd return home and e-mail me with Sacha's response.

⁕ ⁕ ⁕ ⁕ ⁕ ⁕ ⁕ ⁕

A week after Sacha left, the United States began bombing Afghanistan. If I'd found our meager communication wanting in the past, I was finding it downright unbearable this time around. Sirens continued to roar past our apartment day and night, smoke billowed up in a column from the bottom of Sixth Avenue like a giant, wavering tombstone, and the neighborhood was swimming in what would turn out to be utterly futile missing-person flyers.

⁕ ⁕ ⁕ ⁕ ⁕ ⁕ ⁕ ⁕

With hindsight, we can all sum up our experiences of that time succinctly, dinner-party style, but while it was going on, every day, sometimes every hour, seemed to bring a new perspective. Add to that constantly shifting outlook a brand-new identifying trait—married— and an absent brand-new husband who wasn't even a phone call away and you have a woman who went and stuck her head in the sand: I spent day after day in the café across the street from our apartment, a million miles away, writing my first screenplay. It was a romance set in pre-9/11 New York City that allowed me, for five or six hours a day, to escape. Better than reading, I had the power to create exactly, detail for detail, the world I longed to return to.

When I reluctantly emerged from my fictional fog at the end of each day, all I had for comfort was the new ring on my finger. Had our marriage been anchored on flimsy foundations, I might have worried that this tumultuous time apart would drive a wedge between us. Instead, I imagined my ring as one end of a steel (okay, platinum) line connecting me to Sacha, a bond I could display to anyone in our quickly disintegrating world and say, "That man out there? Mine. Thousands of miles and languages and currencies and topographies away, but he's mine. I have official proof that is recognized on every inch of this planet." I'd always been an advocate of same-sex marriage, but now I felt in my gut what it meant to have that piece of paper in hand, and how it would be nothing short of a nightmare to be denied one. There are times, especially in the uncharted waters of early marriage, when that paper is all you have.

Sacha returned safely from that trip and we finally got started on married life under the same roof. He began working at his new job, I finished my screenplay, we stopped wearing contact lenses, because the grit that drifted up to us from Ground Zero meant constant eye irritation. We went out, we ordered in, we held up thank-you signs on the West Side Highway to flash at the endless caravan of construction vehicles. We read books, we went to movies, we wondered whether New York City had a future.

A bond that began to form during wedding planning strengthened during these months. To survive caterers, florists, and even our wonderful parents, Sacha and I had developed a mantra: Us Against The

World. I know this sounds like an antagonistic way to go about the sugary business of nuptials and life in general, especially when you consider that our parents are among our favorite people in the world—a reasonable, lovely quartet who shared the same ethics and aesthetics with each other and us. But even reasonable, lovely people will sometimes focus on details you do not care about, like, say, the menu, or the color of the flowers, or the quality of the hotels in which they are going to house their relatives.

Letting us form a new bond, sometimes against them, was the greatest gift they gave us—graciously conceding their spots to the upstart newcomer marrying their precious child—and one that was indispensable during that first year as husband and wife, when our world was unnavigable. Part of early marriage is learning to put someone ahead of your parents, as painful and unsettling as that may be for those of us who come from tight, happy families. (It's anyone's guess whether I'll manage to be half as merciful to the people my children marry. I practice acceptance now, while they are three and six, to get a running start.) We began to see ourselves as one entity before the wedding; the tragedy that surrounded us during our first year cemented that perception.

Seven months into marriage, Sacha traveled again, only this time it was to lecture on a cruise up the Orinoco and I got to go with him. Instead of bags of rice, there was a chef on board reported to have been snatched up from a three-star hotel in Paris and there were seven kinds of cake at dinner every night. Seven. I'm not exaggerating and my memory has not dimmed (someday scientists will discover a lobe of the brain charged entirely with remembering significant meals). We set sail on a large yacht with seventy passengers who had paid to see the wonders of South America during the day and be enlightened by my husband and his PowerPoint show at night.

One evening aboard the ship, the schedule of events was reversed. After dinner, everyone gathered in the lecture room to learn what we might see on our night excursion into the tributaries of the river. We were to explore the moonless, riparian wilds in Zodiacs. Zodiacs sound like they should be impenetrable and, to my mind, metal modes of transport, but in fact they are inflatable dinghies with motors. Inflatable. Did I mention inflatable? The seats were precarious perches along the edges of the craft. We held flash-lights and headlamps. Everyone else looked for crocodiles. I looked *out* for crocodiles.

I am not as brave as Sacha. Sure, I went the drug-free route with childbirth, but tolerating pain, when you know that you are not in danger of irreparable physical harm, is very different from putting yourself in a situation with unreasonable creatures, where the jungle equivalent of an episiotomy is not in the offing. Most ecologists are lured to their profession, in part, by the inherent adventure. Take Sacha's boss, for instance, who was with us in the Zodiac. She leaned out over the boat and wrestled something in the water. It came up flailing and splashing in the dark.

"Oh, it's a baby," she cooed.

Baby crocodile.

She clamped one hand over its mouth so that we could touch its writhing body. Everyone else in the boat eagerly leaned in to stroke the wet scales, while I screwed up my courage. Since having children, especially a daughter, I have forced myself to overcome instinctive wimpiness in these situations and do the required touching of befanged wild creatures. I didn't yet have to be a role model that night in the Zodiac, but I did have a choice to make: reveal my fear to my brand-new husband or attempt to overcome it for his sake. Why? To show him my intention to rise, over the course of our marriage, to his level of adventurousness, and not sink him to my level of overcaution. To reassure him that just because I had the ring, I wasn't going to suddenly strand him with an unadventurous mate. And yet there was something about the ring that made me less concerned with what he'd think of the result of my test of courage. Reader, I failed to coddle the crocodile.

If the first year of marriage is about realigned loyalties, it is also about the blinders that necessarily come off as you gaze eye to eye at your new Numero Uno. Sacha and I have talked openly—though not too frequently—about our disappointments in each other, there being one significant trait (and any number of small peeves) in the other that we wish was more or less pronounced, or something we'd envisioned ourselves doing more or less of because of the influence of our future partner. For him, it is a longing for a mate who would get him back-packing, camping, and rock climbing more than naturally occurs to me to do. (Tough luck for him; I found this great guy who does that for me.) In that first year, coming to terms with the reality we'd committed to—versus the ideals we'd conjured when we were younger—must have been scary for Sacha. For me, the unease was outweighed by the comfort of commitment; there is something to be said for the reassuring heft of a ball and chain.

. . . .

Ten years ago, like New York City itself, my new husband and I had no way of knowing how we would weather the world events in our backyard. But in just one decade of marriage, we have partaken in better and worse, richer and poorer, sickness and health, stasis and change, much of it sampled during that first year. Would our legal union have been different had we not begun it alongside tragedy? The answer may lie in the kind of tragedy: if we'd suffered a personal loss, 9/11 might have tripped us up or slowed us down. But while the horror left me with sweat-soaked nightmares of flaming buildings and unbounded anxiety for the future of our city, the fact remained that we were some of the lucky ones. The people we loved were safe.

So even though we were welcomed home with weapons and weeping, even though we couldn't huddle together in the immediate aftermath, and even though I have to think twice to remember the actual, overshadowed date of our anniversary, 9/11 did not harm our first twelve months. It turned out to be a catalyst, speeding up the best and hardest transformations, driving Sacha and me together with brute force, and forging, yes, I'll risk putting this in print, an indestructible bond.

All the Time in the World

DARCIE MARANICH

The call came one crisp, late October evening. I answered the phone awkwardly, trying to balance the handset between the select few of my fingers not smudged with sticky cinnamon remnants of apple-cake batter. The apple cake was the latest in a parade of experimental desserts I proudly presented my new husband during those first weeks of our marriage, so determined, I was, to fill him in every sense of the word.

My stomach dropped when—as an afterthought—I glanced at the caller ID. By then it was too late; I'd already picked up.

I'd quickly learned that the life of an army wife was anything but predictable. Already, in our short two-month union, my husband had been called away unexpectedly for weekend drills, overnight guard duties, and what I would come to know as surprise piss tests, randomly sprung on a sleeping populous. They called so often to pull him away during those first weeks when I wanted nothing more than to spend long, uninterrupted days discovering the depths of him that, through the eyes of marriage, seemed new and uncharted. Admittedly, there were times when caller ID was unwelcome, and if I could get away with it, I'd let it ring straight through to voice mail. On this particular night I'd been caught off guard, distracted by baking and the sound of John Mayer's voice flowing so smoothly from the speakers of my under-cabinet kitchen stereo.

"Hello?" I answered, reluctance tinting every last curve of the word.

"Mrs. Maranich?"

The title was so new to me; I hadn't yet worn it in. "Yes."

"This is Major Streeter. I'm trying to get ahold of Lieutenant Maranich. Is he available?"

A bubble of lies floated to mind. He's not here. He's sick. Hospitalized. Out of the country. Just plain gone. My conscience took over, though, popping that little bubble of lies and sending them scattering every which way. "He is," I conceded. "Just a sec."

Within minutes my husband would hang up and turn to me, his eyes so burdened with sadness that I knew full well what he was going to say before he said it. We'd spend the rest of that night together but apart, so separately crushed that nothing could build a bridge between his misplaced guilt and my unadulterated despair.

Just two months before, on a balmy September evening with the weight of a monsoon storm still hanging heavy in the air, Jeff and I stood on a hilltop in the Sonoran Desert and made public the love we were convinced was unlike any that had ever come before it. Surrounded by little more than a scattering of saguaros and a handful of loved ones, we took turns speaking aloud the vows we'd written. He promised to cherish me—and my three young daughters—until time ticked its last. I vowed to him my undying love and unwavering commitment, not having any idea at the time just how quickly my words would be tested.

The phone call that came on that October night served as a two-week warning that Jeff was being deployed to Iraq. The days that followed were both a gift and a curse—time alternately zooming past or dragging on, though the inevitable loomed like a dark cloud all the while.

On his twenty-sixth birthday, I shaved his head almost completely bald at his request. The girls and I sang while he blew out the candles on his lemon Bundt cake. He unwrapped my one gift to him: a framed picture that played my voice at the push of a button.

Early the very next morning we drove to the airport. I sat in a chair and swallowed hard, pushing back lumps in my throat so thick I thought I might suffocate. The girls busied themselves crawling over him as though he were a jungle gym. As though he wasn't marching off to a war halfway around the world. He stayed with us until he couldn't put it off anymore. I can still recall the sight of him approaching that security checkpoint, turning one last time to blow me a kiss from two fingers.

Coming home to an empty house was difficult. Facing the entirety of his civilian wardrobe left hanging in the closet even more so. Nights trumped all of it, though—our king bed stretching out before me like an insult. So, too, did my subconscious taunt me then, conjuring up sounds that weren't there. One night—a couple of months in—I shot straight up in bed at the sound of the doorbell. My heart raced as I made my way to the front door and peered through the peephole, so sure that on the other side I'd see two uniformed men with a folded flag in their hands. There was nobody there. Never had been.

The mail brought thick envelopes full of pages covered front and back in the familiar slant of his print. I opened my e-mail to find new gems awaiting me each morning, dense with poetic professings of his love. Sometimes he sent song lyrics, or long-since-forgotten punch lines to our two-bit inside jokes. The most rare treat of all was digital pictures of him depicted in a distant land, striking a macho army pose with one of Saddam's palaces rising imperially in the background.

What I hadn't predicted was that the quarrels of young love would reach us, in spite of the distance between us. We fought something fierce. Our heated words most often flew through cyberspace, igniting long stretches of silence between us. It wasn't the typical woes of young married life—money, priorities, sex—that fueled our respective fires; ours were disputes born of frustration and stress. Loneliness and blame. Little stones of it piled up, landing with a sharp ping on my internal points scale. I could almost feel them accumulating there, weighing heavy in my favor. On Tuesday nights as I lugged the trash bin to the curb after dark, sure I was going to step on a rattlesnake or some equally scaly desert creature. *Ping.* Every time I drove alone to the Realtor's office to initial the contracts for the house we were building. *Ping.* Every bill I paid. Every toilet I plunged. Every spider I killed. *Ping. Ping. Ping.*

More than once I questioned whether our marriage would outlast his deployment. Almost without fail his voice was the one of reason, so consistently calm and reassuring—even in the face of mortar and rockets—that I always came away from our arguments shamed by the stubborn impulsivity that left me so weak, especially in contrast to his strength.

Four and a half months after his sudden deployment, Jeff was sent home. The girls and I made T-shirts with catchy slogans: *Welcome*

Home Baghdaddy; Glad You're Back from Iraq. We used window markers to decorate every square inch of exposed glass in our house. We tied balloons and strung banners. We dusted and vacuumed and swept and mopped. I woke up on that final morning and literally pinched myself, just to be sure.

Indeed he came home, bearing only a select few scars from his time away, none of them external. I remember walking alongside him in the parking lot of the mall. A nearby car backfired, sending Jeff instantly to the ground. I laughed at him, protected by the ignorance of safe borders—the bliss of a life uninterrupted by the sights and sounds and smells of war.

During his time away, I had dreamed of us. All five of us. I dreamed of picnics and road trips and backyard barbecues. I dreamed of chatter-filled dinners and evening walks around the neighborhood. I dreamed—I knew—that if only he were home with us, we'd settle into the rhythmic hum of a family as true as there'd ever been. It took me a while to admit, even to myself, that my "if-onlys" were as flawed as a fairy tale. What I'd forgotten to account for was that life with three young daughters—one of whom has Down syndrome—isn't always overflowing with the stuff dreams are made of.

It's not that my girls were a surprise to him. Far from it. He'd known about them from the very start and had, in fact, come prepared to dive headfirst into the treacherous ocean of fatherhood. The only problem being that my girls already had a father. It would take them some time to accept another.

I remember long months of refereeing. Each time Jeff would ask one of them to pick up this or put away that, they'd look to me instead. I could read the questions in their eyes without their saying a word: do I really have to do what he says? He held strong, enforcing rules that I established—rules that had been in place for years and years—yet still the girls would come running to me, hedging that I'd nullify anything he might have said. I never did, even though I sometimes wanted to. I felt torn, as though by siding with him I was betraying their tenuous sense of security in a family they already questioned. I became skilled in the art of trapeze, walking so fine a line all while trying to balance our fledgling little family.

Jeff, meanwhile, struggled with the nitty-gritty. He came home in the midst of my attempts to potty-train my five-year-old special-needs daughter. There really are no words to describe the level of patience such a task requires, so I won't even try. Suffice it to say, though, that the job was a trying one, even for a biological parent. My clean freak of a husband had some major adjusting to do. After so many years on his own, Jeff was unaccustomed to finding toothpaste globs in the sink, muddy shoes by the door, unflushed toilets. He lamented my daughters' bad habits; they resisted his influence. I fought for neutrality.

Not all of the forces against us were internal. In-law issues simmered, constantly threatening to boil over. Whereas my parents adored Jeff, his parents were slightly less than thrilled that their West Point alumnus son had chosen for his wife a divorced mother of three. One without a college degree, no less. My mother-in-law seemed to be eager for our marriage to fail, even going so far as to quietly slip Jeff's cell-phone number to one of his high school girlfriends in a shady attempt to derail us during our make-or-break first year. Jeff would pass that test, much to his mother's chagrin.

It certainly wasn't all bad; there were high points. A camping trip to the Grand Canyon with days spent hiking the rim or jumping from boulder to boulder during a family-concocted game we dubbed "rock tag." We spent that week within the tight quarters of a camping trailer and came away from it all close and "Kumbaya," though I don't rule out s'more sugar highs as a contributing factor. At home, Jeff proved a priceless resource for homework help; it didn't take long for my eldest to realize that while math is my weakness, she was lucky enough to have a resident rocket scientist (literally) on hand for tutoring. And take advantage she did. Weekends at home found us wasting away occasional Saturday afternoons, pretending to be tourists in our own city. There were canyons to explore and trails to hike and museums to take in. We went to the pool, the park, the mall. As we neared the end of that first year, we surprised the kids with a seven-day trip to Walt Disney World, a family-moon to rival all others.

There was an undercurrent all the while, a silent tug that left Jeff and me spinning in circles, though the girls were oblivious. In the months that led up to our marriage, we'd considered and compromised on some of the biggest things couples face, from where to live to what to drive to how much to save. One nagging question went unanswered, though: to have or not to have another baby. It was an issue we saw eye to eye on, each of us with matching hesitations. The problem was that neither the yea nor the nay seemed to outweigh; we were content, but not convinced. We didn't talk about it in front of the girls, but once they were tucked into bed, we'd retreat to our own and lie there in the dark for hours, rallying pros and cons back and forth like the game ball, each hoping the other would drive home a winning point. Once—during a weekend trip to Vegas while the girls were visiting their dad—we paid forty-five perfectly good dollars to a psychic, hoping she would peer into her crystal ball and save us the trouble of deciding. In the end she couldn't tell us anything we didn't already know. Unless, of course, we were willing to part with another fifty bucks, which, by the way, we were not. (Here's the good news:

the answer would eventually come some twenty-three months after we said "I do." Dressed in blue.)

Before our wedding, I had Jeff's ring engraved. It was a surprise to him, one that I almost ruined time and time again because I was nearly too excited to keep the secret. It had been a challenge to sum up so big a commitment in so few characters. Though when they came to me, I wondered why it had taken so long to find them: six such obvious little words. They are printed in perfect script on the inside of his ninety-nine-dollar titanium band: *All the time in the world.*

Throughout that first year, I would summon those words to see me through. During the long, lonely stretch of deployment, they rang like a promise in my ears, pushing me just one day further, one day closer. When his return finally came and the constant conflict between him and my girls wore me down, I wondered if my family would ever be whole again. And then I considered the words and I came to understand that with patience and perseverance we'd get there. When I put those words inside his wedding band, I'd meant them for him. I meant that we'd have all the time in the world for nights of endless passion, knowing glances, and secrets shared. All the time in the world to perfect our blueberry-pancake recipe, take that Mediterranean cruise, grow a garden. All the time in the world to decipher the too much from the not enough and the never gonna make it from the almost there. Time for knock-down blowouts and kissy makeups. Time for lazy days and Indian summers and cold wintry nights. I meant those words as a promise to him, but in the end they came back to me, a little time capsule of truth in the face of my doubts.

I don't recall giving Jeff anything for our first anniversary. We're not one of those gifty couples. Well, not usually. He did get something for me, just the once.

There was a gauze bandage around his ring finger when he came home that day. He took it off to reveal what I still consider to be the most meaningful gift he has ever given me. It was a tattoo he designed himself: two interlocking fish that wrap around his ring finger. The most meaningful gift because even after that roller coaster of a first year, even after the unanswered questions, even after the deployment and the kids and the in-laws, even after all that, he'd do it again. Willingly.

And, for the record, so would I.

Blending a Family

SARAH PEKKANEN

The first time I visited my soon-to-be-husband Glenn's family home in northern Virginia, two things happened. First, I was awestruck by his parents' spotless basement—it looked like the "after" photo in a *Real Simple* magazine intervention. (In my childhood home, the basement was the place to stuff old suitcases, broken furniture, file cabinets bought with great optimism but never actually used to file a single sheet of paper, and, occasionally, unruly small kids.)

I wandered around Glenn's parents' basement like a tourist in an exotic country, marveling over the fresh vacuum-cleaner tracks in the shag carpet. I peeked into the laundry room: no overflowing hampers or mateless socks lurking around like lecherous men looking for a partner in a seedy bar—just a washing machine that looked, incredibly, as if it had been newly polished. I picked up a formal family portrait in a gold frame, thinking about my own family's sole professional portrait: my brothers had gotten into a fight after the photo shoot, and my younger brother chopped my older brother's head out of the picture. My parents glued it back in, but you can still see the faint decapitation line.

But my husband's family photo looked like it could be the advertising insert that came with the frame. Everyone was smiling and color-coordinated, with no threat of an impending beheading. I set down the photo, walked a few feet away, and then the second thing happened: the glass in the frame spontaneously shattered.

I refused to take this as a sign, but maybe I should have.

As a journalist who'd written for newspapers including the *Baltimore Sun* and the Gannett/*USA Today* chain, I was always taught to look for the telling details—the little moments in life that illustrate a larger truth. And in many ways, the basements Glenn and I grew up with neatly (or, um, not so neatly) summarized the differences between our families—differences the two of us would be forced to bridge as we learned to live together.

It sounds like the tagline for a sitcom: Free-spirited, messy girl meets hardworking, organized lawyer. In fact, there even was such a sitcom—*Dharma & Greg*—though Dharma had a better wardrobe than me, and also longer, skinnier legs (not that I'm jealous, Dharma, you little ho). You'd think the solution would be obvious: Have a few kooky fights, then learn to compromise. Keep our house messier than Glenn would like, but cleaner than I'm used to. Roll our eyes over our differences, but learn to laugh about them. And you'd be right. Except for one thing.

If our greatest challenge during our first year of marriage was simply to learn how to bridge the gaps in our respective upbringings—between chaos and order, aggressive spontaneity and steady routines, serendipity and traditions—our relationship might have followed that script. Our issues would rise to the surface regularly, but always be neatly wrapped up inside half of an hour.

But there was another complication I never saw coming. A surprisingly big one that was just as firmly rooted in the messages we'd absorbed from our families during our upbringings. Before I could enter into our marriage as a full partner with Glenn, and begin to blend our own routines and rhythms, I needed to do something important: I needed to learn how to make the transition from being a daughter to being a wife.

A bit more background about my parents: my mother is the kind of woman who goes out for coffee with the stranger behind her in the grocery-store line; once, when I was a teenager, I opened the door on Thanksgiving morning to discover several hungry-looking marines (Mom forgot to mention she'd phoned a nearby base and invited anyone who wasn't going home for the holiday to pop by for dinner).

For the record, my father isn't quite as social—as a writer, he happily disappears into the solitude of his home office for hours on end—but he's not shy. When I was a teenager, he once hugged me on a crowded sidewalk in front of strangers. "Dad," I hissed as I steamed beneath a red-hot layer of pubescent embarrassment, "stop it!" He grinned, then shouted at the top of his lungs, "Who are you, kid? You've been following me around for years, eating my food and demanding rides. I don't even know you! Can you get away from me, please?" as people around us cracked up and I melted into the sidewalk.

To say that Glenn's mother is different from mine is to say that George Clooney doesn't have a lot in common with those lecherous pickup artists who hang around seedy bars (but if you happen to have information to the contrary, could you swiftly forward the name of George's preferred bar to sarah@sarahpekkanen.com, please?).

Here are a few examples: my mother once served Indian food and Domino's pizza for Easter dinner just to liven things up (or perhaps because she'd forgotten to cook). Glenn's mother makes the identical menu for all holiday meals—butternut-squash soup, turkey and stuffing, broccoli, hot rolls, and that Jell-O thing that no one actually eats—and serves it on her own parents' wedding china. My mom forgets to wrap presents, and occasionally forgets birthdays altogether—she once dropped off a Pepperidge Farm cake with candles on my doorstep by way of apology for missing the actual event. Glenn's mother wraps gifts in themed paper at least a week in advance, and she's a fan of extravagant bows and card-giving holidays. The people at Hallmark practically know her by name.

My mother craves action, arguments, change. She'll eat blueberry pie for breakfast, canvass door-to-door for politicians (though she has switched political parties twice in the past ten years), and at the last wedding she attended, she ended up on the dance floor with a group of bridesmaids, waving around her arms and screeching the lyrics to "It's Raining Men."

When I was born, the lone girl sandwiched between two boys, my mother thought she'd created a built-in best friend—a daughter who would be just like her. Evidence seemed to support her assumption: We look strikingly similar, and our voices confuse even my father on the telephone. We have the same straight brownish-blond hair (now aided by Clairol), and we both often laugh so hard that we cry.

And yet, on the inside, we're opposites in many ways. I'm not antisocial, but if I'm around too many strong emotions and conversations, I absorb them like baking soda soaks up refrigerator odors. I crave patches of solitude as strongly as my mother longs for heated political debates. Oh—and I'm allergic to politics.

"All my friends say you're my Mini-Me," my mom has said, repeatedly, in a tone that has ranged from wistful to puzzled through the years. "But on the inside, you're your father."

She'd anticipated more closeness, more confidences, more of a reflection of herself—and yet in a fluke of fate or genetics, everything about us, from the foods we eat to the television shows we like, stretches to opposite sides of the spectrum. Our differences—and, more importantly, our inability to accept them—led to epic clashes during my teenage years. We still hadn't resolved them when I married Glenn at the age of twenty-six.

My mother had immersed herself in helping to plan my wedding, and though we fought over things like her desire to throw me a big engagement party (and my desire not to have one at all), things went surprisingly smoothly. Then came the first year of my marriage. My older brother had been wed a few months earlier, and he and his new bride were living in Massachusetts, a ten-hour drive from my parents' home in Maryland. My younger brother had just moved away to live in New Orleans. Everything was changing.

Now that I have three kids of my own, I can look back and imagine what that stretch of time must have felt like for my mother. She was adrift, unmoored. She'd devoted her life to raising us kids—she was the one who piled all of the neighborhood children into her beat-up station wagon to take us on whimsical adventures, like racing up the steps to the top of the Washington Monument (back when they used to let you do that). Sure, she didn't do much cooking or cleaning—those weren't her priorities as a homemaker—but she spent lots of time with us kids.

I think she was terrified that it was all about to crash to an end—that I'd be swallowed up by my left-brain husband and my new in-laws with their strange traditions and habits, and then she'd lose her last close physical link to her children. Maybe she thought that our differences would finally push us apart for good, now that I was married. It's possible she was secretly worried that I might actually fit better into a family that was slightly less . . . flamboyant, especially when it became clear that my mother-in-law and I had a lot in common, including a love of reading, chocolate, and traditional meals. And so my mom reacted by trying to hold on as tightly to me as she could.

The most striking sign came when Glenn and I arrived at the airport on the way back from our honeymoon. We were exhausted and jet-lagged. We looked around for his father, who had offered to pick us up. Instead, we saw my mother.

"I missed you so much," she said as she ran up and hugged me. She seemed near tears.

Missed me? I thought, blinking in surprise. *But . . . I was only gone for ten days.*

Glenn's father showed up a few minutes later, looking just as stunned to see my mother. I didn't know what to do.

"Should I let my mother drive me home and your dad can take you?" I whispered to my husband. His answer was a surprisingly firm: "No." Glenn sensed what I couldn't—that this was a slippery slope. That if I didn't set boundaries with my mother now, they might be impossible to erect in the future.

There had been little hints that we were heading toward uneasy ground, that my mother was searching for a way to define a new relationship with the married version of me. She lived about a half hour away, yet she'd taken to coming over to our town house without calling first. Not that she wasn't calling, too—she phoned almost every day, then called back if I didn't return her calls quickly. Sometimes her calls came early in the morning, before we'd even woken up

I knew Glenn's instincts were right, so I chatted with my mom for a while at the airport, then got into the car with Glenn and his father. I felt so sad as I watched her walk away alone. I wanted to be in both places at once—to split myself into two—and then I felt a rush of annoyance. I was with my new husband. We were about to walk into our town house for the first time as man and wife. We'd almost certainly see my mother within a day or so anyway; why was she doing this?

Glenn was surprisingly tolerant, but I saw him raise an eyebrow as my mother's voice came across the answering machine again and again, and soon he suggested we set a rule for phone calls: none before 10 a.m. on weekends. My mother, of course, violated the rule about as often as I violated my own curfew as a teenager.

Glenn and I were married in mid-November, and as our first Christmas together approached, tension between my mother and me only increased.

"What's your plan for Christmas?" she asked. It might not have sounded like a loaded question, but its weight would've broken any scale.

Glenn's parents also lived about a half hour away—though in the opposite direction from my parents—so we hatched a plan to be scrupulously fair, since both sets of in-laws wanted to see us. We'd visit both family homes on Christmas Eve. Then, on Christmas Day, we'd drive to one house first thing in the morning, race to the other parents' home for the middle of the day and Christmas dinner, then drive back to the first parents' home for dessert. We'd try to please everyone.

On Christmas morning, we awoke early, packed the trunk of our car with gifts, called our dog to jump into the backseat, and headed out. I think we spent almost as much time on the road as we did at our respective parents' homes that day—especially after we realized we'd left Glenn's father's gift at our town house and had to backtrack for it. At around five o'clock, as we careened around the highway for the third time or fourth, our dog got sick all over the backseat.

We arrived home late that night, grumpy and exhausted, having lost our holiday spirit somewhere on the road. Our car would stink for weeks.

Before we collapsed into bed, I looked longingly at the cozy sofa in front of the fireplace in our tiny living room, imagining another scenario: What if Glenn and I had woken up and come down here, lighting a fire and cuddling on the couch before we headed out for the day? What if we'd taken the time to be a couple before being blended into our families?

That was the moment when I realized I needed to take a stand. I was focusing so much on my relationship with my mother that it was taking away the attention my new marriage deserved. I wanted those kooky fights about cleaning to be the stressors in my marriage, instead of my relationship with my mother.

It was high time, I realized, that I learned to honor myself as a wife as well as a daughter.

It wasn't easy, especially at first. My mother still tried to cross boundaries I wasn't comfortable with, but for the first time, I gave myself permission to gently close the gate in front of her—to make my marriage a priority. I began turning off the ringer on our bedroom phone and waiting a day or so to return her calls. And the strange thing was, the thing my mother seemed to fear the most—that she'd lose me once I got married—never happened. Instead, I stopped getting angry with her. I phoned her because I wanted to, not because she'd already called three times that day. I visited my parents because I felt like seeing them, not out of guilt.

There were still fights and misunderstandings, of course, and times of icy silences and loud arguments—but the year after my husband and I got married, my mother made an incredible suggestion, the sort of spontaneous idea only she could come up with: why not have both families join together for one Christmas dinner?

Glenn and I were nervous at first, but willing to try—and it worked out shockingly well. Despite their many differences, my parents and Glenn's parents actually got along (a few strategically placed glasses of wine and the rapid steering away from any conversations involving politics or religion helped immensely). Glenn's mom brought stuffing and turkey to the meal, and my mom whipped up Tofurky (she was going through a vegetarian phase) and random side dishes like falafel. Glenn and I got to eat dinner without glancing at our watches, worried that we were shortchanging one side of the family.

It was such a success that for many years, until my in-laws moved away, we continued to alternate holidays among all of our homes. Everyone pitched in to cook and clean up, wine flowed freely, and we even started some new traditions, like buying inexpensive joke gifts to throw in a grab bag. And every Christmas morning, Glenn and I took some time just for the two of us, for our own little family, before heading out for the day.

Now Glenn and I have three kids of our own. Our house is messier than Glenn would like it, and cleaner than I need it to be. That's probably the thing we squabble about most. My mother is enormously helpful with my kids, and having her and my father around frequently is one of the biggest blessings in my life—despite the fact that she sneaks them to McDonald's and lets them stay up too late. But we don't fight about it. In fact, we haven't exchanged harsh words in years; my mother has become one of my closest friends. We talk almost every day, and I'm often the one who reaches for the phone to dial her.

When I think back to the shattered picture frame in Glenn's spotless basement, I realize it was a sign, a kind of merging of our two styles. Of our two families, and, first and foremost, of ourselves.

Marriage Changes Things

LIZA MONROY

"WHO TAUGHT YOU HOW TO WASH DISHES?" Emir's voice boomed from the kitchen.

We had barely taken the "Just Married" sign off the back of his rusty blue Sentra, and I was sitting on the black futon in the living room of our West Hollywood apartment, job-hunting online while a *Golden Girls* rerun played in the background. A golf-ball-size lump rose in my throat. In the kitchen, Emir stood over the sink, putting the dish rack's contents back in and drenching the dishes in green liquid soap.

"What's wrong?" I asked.

He handed me the offending plate. A faint trace of Parmesan clung to the edge. I scratched it away. Sponge poised, he reached for another dish.

"It's just this one," I insisted. "These others are fine."

"Look at this place!" he shouted, scrubbing vigorously. "I clean the countertops until they sparkle and you leave coffee-cup rings. My clothes are hanging, yours collect in those horrible little piles on the bathroom floor."

He was right, but I balked and called him OCD. It was an attempt to deny, to myself as much as to Emir, the shame I felt over my seeming inability to distinguish cleanliness from mess. Still, he had seen my rooms since we lived in college dorms. He knew I was no Martha Stewart. Why was it different now that we were married? Sometime after the night we vowed to walk each other's hound dogs and polish each other's blue suede shoes in an Elvis-led ceremony in Las Vegas, something had shifted between us. We were too broke to take a honeymoon, and our "honeymoon period" was not exactly shaping up to be a state of bliss.

I had expected nothing to change. But here we were, an unconventional twosome who suddenly found ourselves filling the most conventional of roles. Marriage, I thought, was not supposed to do this—not to us—but as it turns out, marriage changes things no matter what kind of couple you are.

Also, we were very young. I had turned twenty-two five days before our wedding in November of 2001. Emir was eight months older. Our meet-cute story began when he sat down across from me in class back when we were film majors in Boston. We were paired on a project, and coffees, brunches, dancing, and first sleepovers ensued. On paper, our marriage looked no different from a more "traditional" one. All we had to do, come the day we interviewed with the Immigration and Naturalization Service (the INS), was prove that we loved each other, which would be easy because it was true. As for whether ours was a "real" marriage, if we two consenting adults agreed it was, then wasn't it? Noticing the way we started acting after we tied the knot was what convinced me.

What made us different was that Emir was gay and I knew it when I married him. We were not physically intimate and neither of us wanted to be. We married because he was going to have to leave the country after his student visa ran out. I did not have many friends who knew and understood me the way Emir did. He was my best friend. I didn't want to be without him, and I certainly didn't want to be alone.

The real stakes were for Emir, who came from a gay-intolerant Muslim homeland. (In order to protect his family and identity, it's a place I call Emirstan.) He was determined to find a way to make a postcollege life in the United States. In Emirstan, hate crimes against gay people were no cause for outrage. Shortly after 9/11, new prejudice against young Middle Eastern men plus a difficult economy made finding work (which would earn him a visa) difficult for Emir. I understood his predicament. I grew up with my mother, who worked in the Foreign Service in visa sections of embassies abroad. I knew enough about immigration to realize he would likely have to leave the country if I didn't intervene.

So I asked him to marry me. (I didn't tell my mother. For three years she thought he was my "nice gay roommate.")

Emir and I loved each other and offered each other everything except our bodies. At first, he worried our marriage was illegal, but he came around after I made my case for our union. Was an infertile couple barred from the institution of marriage? Couples who did not want children? What about a celibate couple who enjoyed each other's company but shared distaste for physical intimacy? What about open marriages, where both partners agreed not to be sexually exclusive?

When it came to marriage, it seemed the rule was there were no rules anymore.

People have been arrested for green-card marriages, but no one like us—not a close pair who moved in together and shared their lives as we did. We sang along with J.Lo on road trips, watched *Sex and the City* marathons, went out dancing and for long lazy lunches at the Abbey, our favorite West Hollywood gay bar. We talked late into the night while playing our endless backgammon tournament and drinking white wine. We even had the same career dream: to someday work as screenwriters.

What if, I wondered, *after Emir and I become successful and move into a Hollywood Hills villa, we adopt an entourage of international, multiethnic children and live as progressive-minded citizens of the world? What negative consequences, other than annoying our old college friends, could there be?*

Given our circumstances, I anticipated being married would be no different from an endless sleepover with my best friend. The terms of our union were straightforward: we would share an apartment (two bedrooms), a bank account (I'd still have my own, separately, for personal expenses), and our love of bigger, burly men. (Emir and I, small, dark, and petite, look alike, and are both attracted to our physical opposites.)

And so we swung our hips to "All Shook Up" at the Viva Las Vegas Chapel. I thought things between us would be carefree and easy, just like always.

Emir and I agreed to move to New York City in mid-December, for a fresh start as newlyweds. I planned to keep my car to use for road trips or if we ever needed a quick escape. Emir didn't want to drive to New York—motel sheets and rest-stop toilets repelled him. He wanted to fly. We settled on a compromise. I would drive, arrive first, and apartment hunt. Emir would remain behind, sell furniture and his car, then fly out and join me.

The plan was straightforward; the route, winding. I visited the Grand Canyon and Sedona in Arizona, White Sands and a town called Truth or Consequences in New Mexico. I felt like I was on the lam. I wondered what I was trying to escape from and hoped it wasn't my nascent marriage.

The more I drove, the more uncertain I became.

In the parking lot of a strip mall in El Paso, I was suddenly paralyzed with fear. The unfamiliarity of my surroundings highlighted the circumstances of my life, and I was scared. Everything had become strange. I was married, but I was also young and unemployed, and by the time I got to New York, I'd be broke. (Still seeing myself as totally independent, I wouldn't accept help from Emir even though his father had offered to help us out financially.) What was I doing? I felt claustrophobic in the marriage and agoraphobic on the road. Mostly, I was just overwhelmed and didn't know how to deal. So I turned around. Thinking only of getting back to Los Angeles as quickly as possible, I made a huge life decision for us both. Marriage and moving are two of life's most stressful changes, and it was all too much at once. I had moved emotional confusion into literal territory.

I had to get back, and fast.

That I was returning to L.A. was going to upset Emir more than any scrap of cheese on a plate, so I planned out my own punishment while I was still on the road: I would move out of our L.A. apartment before he could kick me out. Back in a Sedona motel room, I perused the Los

Angeles Craigslist and found a room for rent listed by a guy I had met in a diner once. *Aren't you Cameron from that night at Fred 62's?* I wrote. *What a coincidence,* he replied. The room was mine if I wanted it.

"What happened?" Emir asked when he opened the apartment door.

I could give a million excuses but not one good reason. My stomach was lodged somewhere in my throat. The sky was clear, dotted with stars behind the streetlamps.

We walked down the street to Whole Foods on Santa Monica Boulevard and made our way to the salad bar. Light pop music drowned out the silence between us. We paid at separate registers and went outside to the picnic bench overlooking the parking lot. The concrete glistened in the moonlight as if implanted with diamonds— there, but not for the taking. Neither of us touched our food.

"Couldn't you have thought about it more?" he asked. "How could you not know you didn't want to go to New York until you were halfway through Texas?"

"El Paso isn't halfway through Texas."

"What is this, *Thelma & Louise*?"

He buried his hands in his curly black hair.

"Yes; yes, it kind of is like *Thelma & Louise*. That's exactly what it's like."

"There's no way out? You're cornered and have to drive off a cliff?"

"You're better off without me around messing things up for you," I said. "I found a room in Los Feliz. I'll be out of your way."

"Are you kidding?"

"We'll still be married. My mail will come here, we'll do everything right. I'm not going to back out of my promise. I love you."

I wasn't thinking straight. I needed space to reflect. Ultimately, though, my fear of rejection, that Emir didn't love me anymore after I proved myself so impulsive and unreliable, preempted my leaving. Ashamed of my own inability to commit to anything, even a city in which to live, I felt adrift. The marriage was the one thing that was supposed to make me feel anchored, yet I'd run from that, too. How could I focus on keeping Emir with me when I was barely keeping it together? Why I was moving into a stranger's house instead baffled even me, but now I suppose that given my capriciousness, split-decision making, and propensity to act on whims, I feared it was impossible for Emir to trust me again. I was leaving precisely because I loved him and wanted him to be happy. I still wanted to be married. I still wanted to help him. As long as we had the same mailing address, filed taxes jointly, could answer personal questions about each other, and had both our names on a bank account, he didn't actually need me around.

"You don't have to do this," Emir said. Yes, my return had been unexpected and I'd changed the course of our lives without consulting him, but we could talk through it, come up with a new plan, save money, and move to New York down the line. He wasn't going to kick me out; I was being crazy. Still, I moved into Cameron's with the two suitcases still packed in my trunk from the road trip. Only two months into married life, Emir and I were separated.

· · · · · · · ·

My decision felt wrong from the moment I dragged my suitcases across the foyer of my room in my new random roommate's house. Emir and I were comfortable with each other even when we disagreed; at

Cameron's I hid in my room, feeling too awkward and shy to even start a conversation, not daring to go into the kitchen if he was in there.

Fortuitously, within a week, Cameron announced he had reunited with his girlfriend. He was very sorry to have to ask me to leave, he said, but she was moving back in. The breakup had been the reason he wanted a roommate. Was there somewhere else I could go? Because he needed me out in the next twenty-four hours.

"Honey," I said when Emir answered the phone, "I need to come home."

. . . .

Emir arrived, if not exactly with open arms, at least with a wry half smile. They'd just put up the Christmas decorations, tinsel in Tinseltown. One-dimensional gold bells and shiny green wreaths decked out the boulevard. At Cameron's, Emir helped his wayward wife pack yet again. He zipped my suitcases and we returned home, the separation over, both of us relieved.

In the weeks that followed, though, Emir went out on boys' night without inviting me. Before we were married, I was always invited on boys' night. "I need some space," he echoed. Well, the INS was definitely going to give our marriage the seal of approval now, I thought. We bickered, we weren't having sex, and we picked on each other over towels left on the bathroom floor (mine) and his late nights out partying while I sat on the couch alone playing on the Internet. We struggled to find our equilibrium. Could things ever go back to "normal"? Couldn't we still go out for flirtinis at the Abbey or curl up on the couch with tissues and popcorn for rom-com night? Had negotiating the intricacies of the merging of our lives actually ruined our once-easy relationship?

I found a job at a Beverly Hills talent agency where I filed head shots and sorted mail. Emir stayed up until five in the morning playing the Sims and slept in late. Before, I would hardly have noticed, but resentment slowly built. Five months into marriage, he still wasn't working and I grew weary. What if, now that needing a job in order to stay in the country was off the table, it turned out he didn't want a job? Marriage, I was surprised to find, had also heightened my expectations of what both of us would accomplish. I felt deeply invested in Emir, as if our identities had merged.

He continued going out almost every night and I was jealous. And when I came home from work to find him playing the Sims instead of looking for jobs, I lost it.

"I did this for you!" I shouted. "What are you doing?"

I slammed the door and didn't emerge for several hours, leaving his quiet raps unanswered. When I eventually did, I took a hoodie I'd hung over the back of a chair, put it on, and zipped it up to the neck. The room was too cold. Emir kept the air-conditioning going full blast.

"I may not wash dishes the right way," I said, "but why don't you stay home some nights and hang out with me? Or turn the air conditioner off sometimes?"

"Why didn't you say so? Why did you wait until it bothered you so much?"

I wondered, *Why didn't I?*

"I guess I'm not used to having anyone to 'say so' to," I said.

I turned off the television and sat down next to him. This was just like any married argument about dishes and cleaning and living together. We both slipped into this weird, learned husband-wife type of behavior, a typical lovers' quarrel born of a lack of communication. Emir hadn't mentioned that what I was doing (or not doing) bothered him until it boiled over and he snapped, and I'd unwittingly done the same.

"We have to raise issues the second they come up," I said. "Tension comes from what's left unsaid."

"I'm sorry I yelled at you," said Emir.

"I don't ever want you to feel like I forced you into this."

"I know, sweetie, but you're my wife now." He paused, as if the meaning of the word was sinking in. "And I need to make you happy."

In a so-called marriage of convenience without the sexual intimacy that lends a dynamic of vulnerability and need, the fact that this kind of change happened to us revealed that an adjustment period in which there are gaps between expectation and reality, when you need to get used to each other all over again and in a whole new way, is unavoidable no matter what kind of marriage you have. Instead of the marriage bringing us closer together, Emir and I had each panicked in our own ways and tried to escape, me on the road trip, him in an alternate universe provided by the Sims and house music. In the past, I could have driven in figure eights all over the country and only my mother would have objected, and Emir could have played the Sims until his eyeballs fell out. We were used to running around, but that was before. We had to meet all over again in a new place.

Emir started working at a restaurant and selling spa packages on Rodeo Drive. It wasn't exactly what I imagined for him—my husband, I felt, should have a salaried job with benefits and a retirement package—but he was intent on focusing his energy on the screenplay he was writing. I understood. I wanted the same thing. Our shared dreams had been what brought us together in the first place.

. . . .

Before the end of our first year, Emir and I did move to New York City. We flew—no more road trips. On November 17, 2002, we dressed up and had dinner at a tapas place downstairs from our closet-size Lower East Side apartment. After olives, grilled fish, and salads washed down with sangria, the waiter placed the check between us on the table. Emir grabbed it first.

"Happy anniversary," he said.

"Happy anniversary."

We smiled. We had made it through a strange time and things felt lighter now, as if a fog over us had lifted.

In New York, we developed a morning ritual of getting Mexican coffee from a little shack near our building. The one time I went to the coffee stand without him, the cashier, a friendly Hispanic woman, cheerfully asked me where my boyfriend was.

I laughed. "He's not my boyfriend."

"Oh, thank God you know!" she said. "Here I was thinking, 'That poor girl has no idea her boyfriend's gay.'"

I handed her money. "Actually, he's my husband," I said, picking up the coffees and turning to head home, amused by what surely must have been the shocked expression on her face as she watched me go. I wanted to tell her that not so long ago it was not what I would have expected either.

. . . .

We went to one INS interview, but then Emir won the diversity visa lottery, more commonly known as the green-card lottery. We could have divorced, but didn't.

"Something could still go wrong with your paperwork," I said.

"I like being married to you, too," he replied.

We stayed that way for another year before mutually deciding it was time to move on. Emir and I have other partners now. (Bigger, burly men.) In our early thirties, we're probably the world's only divorced couple still in the planning stages of a long-overdue honeymoon, to Graceland. After all that, we still have a thing for Elvis.

Home Is Where the Husband Is

KRISTEN WEBER

I met the man who would become my husband as a college sophomore. Both of us were part of a group of friends that met weekly to watch *Buffy the Vampire Slayer*. It felt like fate when we learned that we grew up four miles apart from each other on Long Island, although it took attending a college four hours away to finally meet. We bonded over shopping at the same local mall and the random fact that I was from a town without mailboxes. He asked me for a ride home for spring break, neither of us expecting what that simple request would turn into.

We graduated college still very much a couple, but also ready to find our own ways in the real world. I knew Marc wanted to be a television writer, but the jobs he could find in any way related to that field were few and far between. He lived on a friend's couch and delivered scripts at night while I lived at my mom's and commuted on a train into New York City. Our schedules were completely opposite.

Our "dates" consisted of meeting at the parking lot at 5 a.m. for a quick hello among swarms of early morning commuters before I would start my day and he would end his.

I didn't care about Marc's crazy hours or his unsteady work. I blindly supported his dream not really knowing what it would eventually mean for me. In the meantime, I was living my own dream. A lifelong bookworm, I was working as an editorial assistant and slowly but surely working my way up the book-publishing career ladder. I moved into my own tiny studio apartment while he moved up to working in an office instead of out of his car. Neither of us could afford to splurge on fancy dinners or even to take cabs, but we managed to make our own cheap fun, and as long as we were together, we never felt like we were missing anything.

After living on our own for about four years, we found a one-bedroom apartment we could afford in Manhattan's Hell's Kitchen and finally moved in together. We also brought home a pug, which was probably not the best thing to do at the same time as we were learning to coexist as a couple in the same space. Sampson cried almost as much as I did his first few days with us. After a life of total freedom, we were overwhelmed by how much responsibility a dog turned out to be. But he soon weaseled his way into our hearts and became an essential part of our new life—and he really didn't require much more cleaning up after than Marc did, although I never really knew whom to blame all the hair shedding on.

Marc checked coats and took on an assortment of odd jobs to contribute to our household income (in between the more relevant stints he could get in the very small New York City television industry). But even though we came home to each other (and Sampson) at night, in some ways it still felt like we were living a college lifestyle. Both of us were very busy with our own lives and responsibilities. We had separate groups of friends—many of whom were single—and we would hang out with them after work more often than with each other. We had a cozy apartment, a brand-new puppy with health issues that threatened to bankrupt us on almost a daily basis, and every single person we were close to in the world was a short car ride away.

Marc continued to look for work in New York, but the specter of living in Los Angeles always hung over our heads. Or, over his head really, as I was living in denial. We had met in New York and we were both from New York. Our families lived five minutes apart. I was thrilled that the man I chose was one who had roots as strong—and in the same place—as mine.

Reality started to set in when Marc had to go to Los Angeles for a few months during our first year of living together. The job he found was very loosely connected to the television industry but more than anything else he'd been able to find, and we were just happy for him to be receiving a paycheck doing what he loved. It had a clearly defined time line, but still—a long-distance relationship wasn't anything I had signed up for. Our New York City apartment was less charming and more terrifying when I was living there alone. Having a dog that needed to be walked every three to five hours gave me the exact schedule cops warn single girls never to have. Our cute puppy also had serious stomach issues that would often result in us hitting the streets at 3 a.m., and that cute puppy wanted to say hi to every rat that crossed our path. When one afternoon a homeless man told me he'd been waiting a couple of hours for us to walk by on our usual walk, I knew that being a single mom to a dog with a boyfriend a six-hour flight away wasn't what I wanted. I couldn't wait for him to come home.

By the time I turned thirty—and after more than ten years together—my wife clock finally started ticking (blame that on being a child of divorce, if you will). I came home one night to Sampson greeting me at the door with a note on his collar, which led to finding Marc waiting on his knee with a beautiful ring. I couldn't wait to start planning our wedding, complete with a pug ice sculpture and paw prints decorating our wedding cake. But then Marc's dream came true in a way neither of us ever imagined. He finally got the call to be a television writer, and of course the job was in Los Angeles. I ended up planning most of our wedding with my mom, running whatever details I could by him when I could get him on the phone. A three-hour time difference doesn't really work when one person needs to go to sleep before the other even gets out of work or one person is still sleeping when the other one is heavily into their workday. I never imagined I'd be tasting my potential wedding cake with just my mom and grandmother, or designing the menus with a coworker instead of my husband. We hit a low point when I had to send him our wedding-cake design to comment on via fax, although this is probably how I was able to sneak so many pug-themed items into our day.

We had an amazing wedding, but it felt more like a good-bye party, as I knew what was coming next. The minute we came back to New York from our honeymoon, he was on a plane moving to Los Angeles. There were no details on when this job would end, and this time his absence felt like a different ball game. I wanted to start our married life together, and he was embarking on the most exciting time in his career while coming home to a barely furnished, empty apartment. I had never been one to envision the 2.5 kids behind a white picket fence, but I also certainly never imagined starting my life as a wife with my husband not even in the same time zone. I finally knew what I had to do. Two months after our wedding, I quit my job, packed up our pug, and moved out to join him.

Moving to Los Angeles was a shock. I had some vague ideas about embarking on a new career or how this would be some kind of wonderful adventure. But I quickly realized that giving up New York, all my friends and family, and my incredible job was just too much. New York is a place that gets into your blood. I did try to make the best of it, though. We were moving away from the book-publishing capital of the world to a place where saying you're an "editor" results in someone asking you to edit their film reel. I decided to become a freelance book editor anyway, so I could at least continue working in the field that I loved. Unfortunately, being a freelancer can be very isolating in a town where you don't know a soul. Now I was home all day with only our pug to keep me company. And the pug wasn't helping anyone make friends. He was too busy doing a dance of joy that looked more like a seizure whenever we hit grass. People would cross the street to avoid us so I couldn't tell them it was a result of him walking mainly on concrete for years. I was also working in an empty apartment with only an air mattress and a couple of pieces of patio furniture as we waited for all our belongings in the world to make their way across the continent.

During the day, I talked to friends and family in New York and mourned the life I had left behind. There was a whole new life stretching out in front of me, but I didn't want any part of it. I had followed my husband to Los Angeles for his dream, but I felt like all of mine were dying. I had the love of my life, but I just didn't know if that was enough.

I often asked Marc why he hadn't told me moving to Los Angeles was an inevitability when we first met, to which he replied, "There's a reason all the stars live in Hollywood." Hence, the denial. But even if he had made it clear (or even if I had heard what he was saying), that wouldn't have changed anything. I didn't want to be in Los Angeles, but I most certainly didn't want to be anywhere without him. And I realize now that even if he had put Los Angeles on the table as an option from the very first day that we met, I would never have given up him.

Marc and I call that initial period (even if it did last our entire first year of marriage) my black hole because that's really what it felt like I'd slipped into. New York City is a hard place, but it was no match for Los Angeles. I hadn't driven in ten years and was now living in a city where cars were the only option. I avoided the freeways, but trying to find a parking spot or where I had parked my car in a parking garage could drive me to tears. I tried to walk wherever I could—one of my favorite things about living in New York—but like the song says, "Nobody walks in L.A." Crossing the street felt like an intense game of frogger, not to mention all the looks of pity I got from drivers (when they weren't almost hitting me) for not having a car.

In New York City, you're never alone even if you are alone. There are always people out in the street no matter what time of day or night, and I even started to look fondly back at my friendly Hell's Kitchen homeless buddy who kept such a close eye on my dog-walking schedule. But in Los Angeles, everyone is in their own cars on their own schedules doing their own things. It was very hard to meet anyone. And I had a hard time putting myself out there. Trying to meet new people in Los Angeles often felt like I was back in high school, trying to break into the popular clique. I would come home and complain to Marc that I had all the friends I needed in New York and I never thought at this point in my life I would have to start completely over. He would buy me ice cream to cheer me up, and then I realized if I kept whining I'd weigh three hundred pounds.

In New York, I often felt like we were living very separate lives. We only spent quality time with each other a couple of nights a week, if we were lucky. It was much more common for one of us to come home just as the other was getting ready for sleep. I was never one of those women to lose myself in a guy, but we were all each other had in a brand-new city. We were completely on our own, away from everything and anything we had ever known.

Even though I felt sad and lonely, something amazing started to happen. Marc would come home from work, and we would go shopping for furniture. Slowly, our apartment started to feel like home. As we were each other's only friend, once his job ended for the season, we were together all the time. I started to realize that just being with him felt like home. He made an unfamiliar and often scary place feel safe for both me and our pug. I had taken care of him a lot during our relationship while he tried to establish his career, but now he was taking care of me.

And then somehow, the sun came out—literally. There's nothing quite like Los Angeles weather. Plus, we were having so much fun exploring our new city together. We acted like true tourists, keeping our eyes peeled for celebrities and even taking a couple of Celebrity House Tours. We loved going to the movies in Hollywood, where the person sitting next to us might actually have worked on—or appeared in—whatever we were seeing. We bought annual passes to Disney Land, and I loved that we could pop over there and ride the Haunted Mansion or Pirates of the Caribbean whenever we wanted to. I loved being so close to the beach, and being able to hike through breathtaking canyons instead of just to the subway. I realized that being with your perfect other person can be all that you need, no matter where you are.

I had been with Marc for over thirteen years, but it took moving across the country during our first year of marriage to really become a couple.

Faith and Fairy Tales

ANDREA KING COLLIER

Once upon a time there was a young couple who was, well, picture-perfect, at least to the human eye. As happens in most stories that have a handsome prince and a cute, resourceful princess, they got married in an over-the-top fairy-tale wedding. There was a big dress, a bigger cake, big drama, and four hundred guests.

In hindsight, there was big dumbness. At twenty-six years old, I was so focused on the ring and the dress and the man of my dreams that I didn't see what we know happens in almost all fairy tales. I wandered into marriage without a single thought about the wolf in the woods that would huff and puff and threaten to blow our house of new straw and no foundation down.

There was no planning for what happens when an only child (me) tries to build a life with someone with a big family (him). There was no planning for the arguments that would spring up out of the most ordinary things, like buying chicken already boned and skinned, or who gets to control the remote. Each, a minor struggle, but for two people who were totally unprepared for the delicate dance of negotiation and compromise that marriage requires, together they added up and got overblown. Not only was the marriage brand-new, but we had to figure out how to be grown-ups.

No. We couldn't see ahead to the friends and family who would innocently or sometimes not so innocently wreak havoc in our lives. There were the arguments about his siblings or friends just dropping in without calling, or the chaos that ensued because I didn't set up the spices in the same way his mother did. Each thing benign by itself, but together all the little things signaled that the honeymoon was definitely over.

The first year was a thousand-piece puzzle of sorts. Even though we thought we knew each other inside out before we got married, we had to piece together what it meant to be committed for the long haul. He struggled to understand a woman who couldn't balance a checkbook to the penny, and I couldn't understand why a man wore his old pants until you could see through the butt.

These are the things that didn't get dealt with before we said, "I do." They didn't go away, they just boiled in the cauldron, like a witch's brew. They just showed up each and every time someone left their socks in the floor or forgot to take the groceries out of the car— even decades later. The things we didn't know needed to be cleared off the table in the beginning, before the wedding, like who's family got us at Christmas and who got us at Thanksgiving, would become little bricks in the foundation of our marriage and our fights.

I was also challenged by a bout of depression, probably triggered by the loss of the grandmother who raised me. My husband would come in and ask what we were eating for dinner, and I would run into the bedroom in tears. He was confused by the sadness—after all, we got married, didn't we? That's what I wanted, wasn't it? I didn't know how to say that I had built an unrealistic fairy tale of a marriage in my mind, and we were not living up to it. In hindsight, I know that nobody could live up to that.

In real life, the first year is as perilous as any obstacle that the Brothers Grimm could imagine. And if you are lucky, you actually fundamentally like each other, because even that gets tested from time to time.

Almost everything that could happen in that first year did test us. He lost his job. I quit mine. We were broke as hell for the first few months, which is what happens when neither of you has a job. Someone robbed our house and stole our televisions, video recorder (it was thirty years ago), and our ice cream out of the freezer, in the very first week after the wedding. We moved—twice, including almost having to move in with one of our parents. It was like we banked up a whole lifetime of crappy stuff in twelve months.

It is easy in marriage, when life is throwing you all kinds of monkey wrenches, to forget that you love each other. Even the smallest thing, like going to the grocery store together, would spiral into a major fight. He didn't know what to do any more than I did. Plus he was a guy. Sometimes he just wanted to be by himself to put on some headsets and listen to some jazz.

I couldn't wrap my little princess brain around the need for alone time (something that marriage and little kids would correct) and saw it as a personal rejection of me. My mind went to all my insecurities.

Wasn't the whole point of marriage to be together ALL THE TIME? What was wrong with me? Why wasn't I enough for him? Maybe he didn't really love me if he wasn't willing to go shopping with me or kiss me every time he left the room.

Or were we just two people in love, who might not be able make it work? In truth, I did love him so much that it scared me. All of my fears bubbled to the surface, forming a frothy toxic spill over everything that was important to us. Sometimes he could see it in my eyes, and say, "It's going to be all right. I promise." Sometimes I believed him.

Although we believe in God and good, neither of us is a religious person. Yet it was a real faith, a belief that we were really supposed to be together, that kept us hanging on. The first time I saw my husband I was out on a date with someone else, and I spotted him across the room. There was this voice inside me that said, *That's going to be your husband. Take a good look.* Call it my God voice, or my too-many-glasses-of-wine voice, it was clear, and confusing. I'd thought the guy I was out with was going to be my husband. It would be another three years before I even saw him again, or even knew his name. But the first thing I remembered was that this voice told me who this man was going to be in my life.

Faith. Belief. Trust. I believed that God wanted him for me. I still do. You just don't look a gift horse in the mouth, especially if the gift came from something greater than you. If there hadn't been that underlying faith, I am sure that I would have thrown in the towel at about six months. And that would have been tragic, because we wouldn't have made it to see it get better, great, terrible, and then wonderful again. In order to have a real marriage, you have to stay married.

Having faith that you are where you are supposed to be, when all else fails, is a good thing. And it really came in handy in the first year when I took some money my mom gave me as a Christmas present and bought a few pairs of shoes (fifteen), and he got mad and bought a rusted-out old MG sports car with his hidden emergency savings account. My Prince Charming turned into a beast that sucked all the life out of me. And I in return became some screeching harpy who started every sentence with "You never," or "I hate when," or "I just hate you."

During the time that we were both out of work, our routine was to get up in the morning and stake out our spots on the couch in the living room. We'd watch the *Today* show, and go through all the ABC soaps, and on to the evening news, with breaks for lunch or snacks. Thank goodness we both liked *All My Children* and *General Hospital*. I recently asked him about how he saw our first year, and he says those days on the couch were fun. "Don't you really think that it was good?" He also remembers fondly the fact that I would cook three square meals, make pies, and grind my own hamburger meat. "Why don't we grind hamburger anymore?" he asked.

After three months of soaps and soufflés and unemployment, we both got jobs, moved, and found a house to rent. We were the first of our crowd to have a real home. And I was the only person in our age group who actually liked to cook. So our house became a hub where our friends, even the married ones, could get a home-cooked meal without going to their mother's. After a few months of relative bliss and traditional living, we decided to throw our first dinner party. It was a real grown-up party, with food that I cooked, good wine, and music. I used the china, crystal, and silverware we got for the wedding. And for that moment I think we were impressed with being married. I was happy until his brothers, who I had insisted not be invited, showed up. They snuck out of the garage with half of my food and all of our liquor. My husband shrugged and said, "You don't understand because you are an only child. That's what brothers do." He explained that when you marry a person you marry their family, warts and all.

"Do you do that?" I asked, afraid that this was something else I didn't know about him.

I just remember being so stressed out and overwhelmed that I passed out on the floor. The good news was that I didn't have to explain to our guests what happened to the food and drinks. The party was over after that.

My husband was right. I didn't understand nor did I have anybody who could help me figure it out. I soon learned that there is nobody you can really talk to about YOUR marriage, so it is best to keep your mouth shut. There should be a law. A newlywed should be banned from talking to other newlyweds—or for that matter anybody who hasn't been married for a hundred years. Maybe they can talk, but they shouldn't talk about their marriages. Given a frozen margarita, some good guacamole, and a little marital discontent, nothing but mayhem can ensue. Debriefing about the horrors of snoring and old girlfriends, and in-laws, without any context or life experience in navigating out of those troubled waters, isn't helpful.

Sure it makes you feel as if you are not alone. But it also makes you wonder why anybody ever got married or stayed that way. Real conversations should be limited to women who are marital survivors. Would you expect answers about surviving job loss, breast cancer, a train wreck, or a hammertoe from a person who has no experience in surviving these things?

. . . .

Even if I talked to my mother about most things, talking to her about my fragile young marriage made it worse. She could be angry and passive-aggressive about her own marriage to my stepfather, and always gave me angry and passive-aggressive advice, even though she really did love my husband. The minute any marital pearls of wisdom came out of her mouth, even I knew I shouldn't do it unless I was ready to wave the white flag and call it done. "Don't be a fool for some man," she'd say.

Women. Before the wedding, they are cheerleaders. Making you feel like an old maid for not being married yet. They point out all the fun you are missing. Yet not one of them tells you just how challenging the first year of marriage can be, until you are waist-deep in it. Of course, I wouldn't have listened, because we all think that we invented a new kind of love, which is so musical and magical that it couldn't possibly be anything other than happily ever after—every single day.

But I would have appreciated it if someone had just said that the first year is the thing you have to go through to get to the happily married part. Even if you have a first year that is one extended honeymoon period, it's only the cocktail hour/warm-up and you've yet to sit down for the entrée/actual show. For me, the first year was like being rodeo riders. I had to muster just enough faith to hang on until the ride got smoother. Sometimes the frog turns into a prince, and on some days he goes back to being a frog. And sometimes Cinderella's glass slipper gives her blisters, and she gets really cranky. Even though it was scary and awful and there were lots of red eyes and wolf breath and big teeth, this girl and the boy managed to go on to live their version of happily ever after—so far.

The notion of true romance and a love deluxe just gives you something to hang on to while you're fighting or not fighting. Nobody tells you the whole fairy tale, so in the first year, there have to be lots of little leaps of faith.

At least I had faith that if we just hung in there, our marriage would survive. Many of our friends who had gotten married a year or so before me were falling down the rabbit hole. My husband and I had an unspoken agreement that no matter how angry we might be at each other, we never brought it out of our home. We had witnessed enough screaming matches among our friends to know that that was not how we would present ourselves to the rest of the world. All around us, there were divorces, near divorces, and things that should have caused divorces in that first year. Then there was one couple of friends who didn't actually get divorced but lived together for about a year and never saw each other again. Not everybody got divorced, but everybody we knew was suffering the growing pains of learning how to be a married couple. It took me years to figure out that for most of us, it's a part of getting to know each other and yourself in this new construct called WE.

The couple that swore that they were so happy, I found out later, was lying. They wove big elaborate stories about how blissful they were, and how they loved to see each other come into the room. And "what is the secret to your success?" those of us who believed them asked. Lots of sex, the wife would slyly answer. Now, this was a problem answer for those of us in the know. There was, in fact, lots of sex, but we later found out that 80 percent of it was being had by him, outside the marriage.

I am still surprised at how little "long-marrieds" tell you about what it is going to be like in that first year. And it is even more fascinating that they all have the same doofus piece of advice: NEVER GO TO BED ANGRY. I am angry that people told me that. It is so, well, so not helpful. Of course you are going to go to bed angry. Maybe a better piece of advice is "try not to go to bed angry every night for two consecutive months."

In the world of the fairy-tale marriage, telling someone to never go to bed mad is like telling Cinderella to get home before the coach turns into a pumpkin. Or it's like telling Snow White, "Girl, you better not eat that apple." You know it isn't going to happen. If someone had only told me to forget that dumb advice, and instead told me how take a deep breath before I said the things that I would be horrified that I said decades later, that first year would have gone a lot smoother.

In the first few months, I tried. I just wouldn't go to bed. I'd want to stay up and talk it out. If it took three days of spinning in circles and talking about long-gone girlfriends and the fact that he is inconsiderate in leaving the toilet seat up, then I thought we ought to talk it out. After all, real grown-ups with real marriages that lasted longer than fifteen minutes told us never to go to bed mad.

It wasn't practical advice. It was aspirational advice. If I had been a better, more Belle version of myself, I would look at the Prince/Beast version of him and say, "What the hell."

Somewhere near the end of the twelfth month, I got sick and tired of being sick and tired. And he got tired of hearing me scream and wail and cry. The fairy tale that never was gave way to faith that we should really be together. We sat down and talked about everything we had been through, and realized that even though that first year huffed and puffed, it didn't blow our marriage down. We started to remember that before there was a fairy-tale wedding, there was a friendship. Even though it didn't seem like it, we really liked each other and didn't want this roller-coaster first year to ruin it. During the conversation, he got up and left the room, coming back with his only pair of shoes in his hands. "Do you think you could show me how to buy some shoes?" he said, with that sheepish grin that I loved. As if it was totally involuntary, a hootlike noise came out of my mouth. It was so startling and unrecognizable, it was laughter. Then he laughed. And this one little gesture clicked in a release—we laughed until we cried. With all the death and destruction, I had lost an essential tool for any relationship—a sense of humor. It felt good; no, glorious. And at that moment it became the unspoken agreement that we would find a reason to laugh, every single day.

The first year was impossible. The second was hard. The third one led to parenthood for the first time. The eighth year brought us a second child. There have been deaths of parents and siblings, lost jobs, and found careers. That first year was the first rung of the ladder, the bottom stair, the starter's block. It was the once upon a time in a far faraway land of two really young people who didn't have any magic wand or playbook. We didn't know any spells. There was no wise old sage ushering us to the happy ending. It was a decision we made every day. There were some days that I'd say, "I love you," in the morning, when all had I wanted to do was smother him in his sleep the night before. Then there were others that I would watch him sleep and be so filled with love for him, it would give me a lump in my throat. Never a dull moment.

In the end, it was more about faith than the fairy tale. It was about a belief in the voice that introduced me to my husband. I was the girl looking for the dream, learning that this one would require work and patience and love. Before him, I spent a lot of time singing "Someday My Prince Will Come." And when he showed up, I had to learn how to love him, and to let myself be loved by him. Now every night I look at him and think about the ups and downs of our life, and every morning I think about our love and family, and am ever grateful for faith that got us through when the fairy tale wasn't enough. Twenty-nine years later, I feel like we've got the happily ever after.

WE ARE SO GOOD TOGETHER

Ciao, Baggage

CATHY ALTER

They just kept going around and around on an endless loop, the same red knapsack, green duffel bag, and bungee-corded brown box circling the room like refugees stuck on a Ferris wheel. My husband Karl's suitcase appeared immediately, loaded with Etro striped shirts, Ferragamo loafers, and his prized Dries Van Noten sport coat. But after two hours of waiting, frantically jumping from one baggage carousel to another as a smattering of arriving flights touched down, it became painfully clear that I would be spending the next ten days in Italy stuck with the clothes I had on my back: a BO-infused green T-shirt with a pink heart silk-screened across the front, a pair of jeans that were decorated with various in-flight meal mishaps, and highlighter-yellow slipper-sneakers. Not even my carry-on bag could save me—all it contained, besides my wallet and passport, was a handful of Dramamine, a horseshoe-shaped neck pillow, and a dog-eared copy of Thomas Mann's appropriately titled *Death in Venice*.

It wasn't like this the last time Karl and I were in Italy. Two years earlier, I had an entourage of luggage when we made our way from Rome to the Amalfi coast to attend the wedding of Karl's good friends Eric and Shana. Back then, my multiple bags were jammed with everything from the filmy peignoir set I had planned to pull out on our first night in Rome to the full-length judge's robe I had volunteered to transport to Positano, a favor to the officiant (who later admitted he wanted the extra space in his own suitcase for a postwedding shopping spree in Milan). Instead of asking myself, *Do I really need all those shoes?* I told myself as I demolished my apartment in a state of packing frenzy, *You'll be ready for anything*—from a freak snowstorm to the sweltering heat that this new love held for me.

Of course, all this overzealous preparedness was probably a way of managing my anxiety, a belief that as long as I packed that pair of silk cargo pants, those fourteen tubes of lipstick, and, I'm embarrassed to admit now, a spare roll of toilet paper, I'd somehow manage to avoid another kind of travel emergency, one where my new boyfriend decided he didn't really care for my company after spending five consecutive days with his plus-one wedding date. Karl and I had been seeing each other for only a few months, and up until our Italian getaway, we had spent only a handful of weekends together, lolling around in bed or on one of our respective couches watching reruns of *Family Guy*. This trip required putting on actual clothing and remaining upright for an extended period of time, negotiating territory beyond our regular haunts in D.C., and sharing a bathroom with a handheld showerhead and a door that did not lock or do much to block out certain, er, noises. It could be, as a friend so helpfully noted the night before my departure, "a make-it-or-break-it test of our relationship."

As it turned out, weddings in countries with sun-dappled piazzas, hushed Byzantine passageways, and copious amounts of red wine are more of the "make it" variety. I spent most of the week crying tears of insane joy. Practically everything made my heart swell to Hallmark proportions: eating fresh fruit on the tiny balcony of our room in Rome, wandering around Pompeii and giving our own made-up tour ("Over here you'll see some ancient toilets," and "This was once considered Toga Alley") when we strayed from the group, buying forty-ounce bottles of Peroni and drinking them on a scrubby patch of land while cars and scooters whizzed by and the sun set behind the Colosseum. "Oh crap," I'd say every time the waterworks began. To which Karl would respond, "What have you done to me?" before cupping my face in his hands and looking at me like the romantic sap we both knew he was becoming.

I was deliriously happy because I knew what it was like to be so profoundly unhappy. Before Karl, I had been married to a guy who was so wrong for me, my parents actually phoned a week before the wedding and told me it wasn't too late to call things off. ("I could have had my eyes done!" my mother later complained, annoyed that she had forgone an eye lift in order to pay for what she called my "starter marriage.") I spent the entire five years of marriage trying to prove everyone wrong, impressed by my fortitude even as I turned inward and old, an angry stranger to myself and a sad nuisance to friends.

But in Karl I had found someone who finally made sense. Handsome and forthright and predictable in a way that was a lifesaver after my gay-divorcée haze of bad decisions, Karl adored me for the precise reasons for which I wanted to be adored. He listened intently to early drafts of stories and laughed uproariously in all the right places. When I brought home a teaching award for distinguished professional achievement, he told me I was the prettiest genius he knew. And when my head became hot with sleepiness, he would lay his palm across its crown and say, "Sometimes I see you as a little girl."

Is it any wonder that Italy—a boot that seemed custom-made just for us—became the embodiment of every four-hankie chick flick I had ever seen?

I bawled the hardest on our last night. Karl and I had begged out of the postwedding group trip to Capri and rushed back to Rome, our Rome, where we strolled the fancy streets near the Spanish Steps and ate dinner al fresco with the Parthenon as our background. "I don't want to leave," I sobbed on the steps of a church, flat on my back and staring up at the stars. Returning to Washington meant reentering our real lives, held in separate beds, compromised by the demands of work and abandoned friends, a burning relationship essentially watered down on American soil. In my ideal world, Karl and I would remain joined at the hip.

"We'll come back," Karl said, gently cradling my head against the cool church steps. "You'll see."

And we did come back, deciding to celebrate our first year of marriage in the country where we fell in love. It didn't escape me that the last time we were in Italy had been to witness the marriage of our friends and now we were back to celebrate our own, and I fully appreciated the trip's symmetry.

Of course, I wanted to pack accordingly. We would be kicking things off with four days in Florence, new territory for us, and wrapping things up in Rome, a welcome-back tour of our burgeoning romance. And even though I was no longer packing to manage my nutty relationship jitters—the ring on my finger pretty much took care of that—I realized that successfully subjugating that anxiety had freed up way more space in my suitcase for extra shoes, among other (plenty of other!) things.

So when we arrived in Florence and my luggage did not, I was concerned it would be hard to repeat the same romantic glow of our past trip dressed in dirty jeans and a sweat-stained T-shirt. This was not the chic image I had of myself parading up and down the Via Veneto.

"Don't worry," Karl said as we joined the line of other passengers in similar luggageless states. "I'm sure your suitcase will show up tomorrow."

Not to insult the way things work in Italy (Berlusconi has pretty much roped that cow), but after a lot of hand gestures and mounds of paperwork (helpfully prepared in Italian, a language I can only order in), I had little confidence that my luggage would arrive in time for our golden anniversary.

I spent my first night in Florence eating a slice of pizza on the curb and washing my underwear in the sink. "You'll see," said Karl, happy my nightgown was still lost in transition, "we'll wake up and all your clothing will be waiting for you."

But they weren't waiting for me the next day. Or the day after that. When I passed through the lobby in exactly the same outfit I'd had on the day before, I wondered if the beautiful pair working the front desk turned to each other and muttered unkind things about my pre-dilection for shirts with giant pink hearts on them. Out on the streets, I felt dirty and obvious, and even though there were plenty of fanny packs and Bermuda shorts on view, all I saw was a city of Versaces and Valentinos.

But I made do, sharing Karl's toothbrush and deodorant and shampooing the ripeness out of my clothing. The hotel provided me a kit containing a plastic comb, dental floss, and a shoe chamois. There's a classic book called *Europe on 5 Dollars a Day*. Well, forget that. I was rewriting my own version, surviving on just five items a day.

Of course, Karl encouraged me to go shopping for a new wardrobe. "I'll buy you anything you want," he said, leading me into a shop filled with crisp, neatly stacked blouses and perfectly cut linen trousers. I made a beeline for an ivory-colored shirtdress and held it against my body. I hadn't been clad in anything other than what I had on when we left Washington, and suddenly, standing in front of the mirror, I saw myself in something that was clean and pressed and pretty.

"Go and try it on," urged Karl. "I bet it will look amazing."

If being married to Karl had taught me anything, it was to be optimistic. His hope sprang eternal every day and his unshakable belief that everything would turn out fine in the end had an amazing effect on a born-and-bred worrier like myself. Instead of adding to my anxieties, Karl's capable hands took them away.

"I'm sure my luggage will show up tomorrow," I told him, replacing the dress on its hook and thinking of my own perfectly amazing one, packed between my black cardigan and palazzo pants.

"Are you sick with fever?" joked Karl, using the back of his hand to feel my forehead. "You're actually refusing a new outfit?"

"If I get the dress, I'll have to get the shoes," I countered, looking down at my sneakers. "And you know how impossible it is for me to find shoes that fit my narrow feet."

The truth was, I was beginning to love the freedom that being clothesless afforded me. Every morning, instead of wondering what to put on, I just put on the exact same thing and spent the extra time reading the guidebook. I didn't even have a pocketbook, deciding at the last minute to pack my feedbag-size Isaac Mizrahi in my luggage. Now, instead of digging around for a compact to powder a shiny nose, I let my nose be shiny. Instead of applying lipstick after every meal, I left my lips alone. Instead of being elbow deep looking for my sunglasses, I just squinted into the sun's reflection off the Arno River. It took a day or two to get over the initial "Oh no, someone stole my bag" panic and the muscle memory of tossing my five-pound Mizrahi over my arm. But once I acclimated, I discovered there was no better feeling than crossing the Ponte Vecchio with both arms swinging light and free.

Walking around so unencumbered freed me in other ways as well. Instead of worrying about what I didn't have, I became much more aware of what I did have. Here was a guy who didn't care if my pits stank like hard cheese or my hair didn't bounce and behave. "I feel like we've known each other for years," Karl had said early into our marriage, "and now we're just catching up." We had spent our first year doing just that, seeing each other at our worst, me with a death-defying flu and he, immobile for weeks with a broken knee and pee bottle that needed constant emptying. We had also shared all those glorious dreams that all newlyweds surely think of: a starter house, our first family Thanksgiving, the sweet delight of a new baby.

We spent our last night in Florence eating salted bruschetta and pasta with wild-boar ragout on the terrace of a fancy restaurant overlooking the Arno. Karl took a photo of me and handed the camera across the table. The resulting image startled me. With my naked face and hair pulled back into a loose ponytail, I had unwittingly mastered a look of effortless cool. With my glass of red wine raised to the camera, I also looked ridiculously content.

The next day, on the train to Rome, I was one of the few passengers who didn't have to wrestle any belongings into the narrow overhead baggage racks. We passed the time reviewing the photos we had taken in Florence.

"You look like one of those Roaming Travelocity Garden Gnomes." Karl laughed.

It was true. With my lone outfit, it looked like I had been cut and pasted in front of all the standard tourist attractions. There I was, the human gnome, waving in my green-and-pink T-shirt on the Ponte Vecchio, posing with pigeons in front of San Lorenzo, standing on line at the Accademia to meet the *David*.

"If my clothes don't show up soon," I noted, "people are going to think we covered all of Italy in a single day."

Rome was exactly as we had left it. We retraced our steps, eating dinner at Da Fortunato, the place by the Parthenon we had loved so much, window-shopping, hand in hand, along the Via del Babuino, making out among the tumbled columns of the Forum.

"Nothing has changed," said Karl. We were sitting on plastic chairs at one of those irresistible tourist traps that line the perimeter of the Piazza Navona.

"Just like my outfit," I quipped.

"Well," Karl continued, pulling his chair closer to mine. "One thing has changed since the last time we were here." He took my left hand and twirled the platinum band that encircled my ring finger. "Now you don't have to cry about going home."

"Why's that?" I asked, although I already knew the answer.

"Because now you're stuck with me." He winked.

I reached over and tugged on his band, which was made out of titanium and a thin band of platinum. Karl once told me he loved hearing the sound his ring made when he tapped his left hand on a hard surface.

"That's what I like best about being married," I told him.

My luggage arrived the last day we were in Rome, looking like it had spent the week being kicked around by the American Tourister gorilla. Inside, I knew, were all the outfits I had imagined wearing— my Pucci minidresses and stacked-heel sandals, my Capri pants and boatneck sweater, my prized denim skirt and ballet flats. There were mounds of clean underwear, an army of rolled-up T-shirts, and enough scarves to start a magic act.

"My apologies for your inconvenience," said the concierge, an earnest woman with a neat brown bun and tightly laced oxford shoes. We had come to check in with her daily with the simple shorthand of "Anything?" To which she would reply, *"Proprio niente."* Nothing at all.

As Karl and I wheeled past her, she turned and asked, "How did you do without all your lovely things?"

"Actually," I told her, "I had everything I needed."

Animal Husbandry

CLAIRE LaZEBNIK

Going into therapy as an adult is useful because it forces you to realize that the values of the family you grew up in aren't necessarily universal, that the world is full of options, and that you should break free of any inculcated mythos that claims there's only one right way to do things.

Another way to figure that out? Get married.

When you join your life with someone else's, the way you've always done things and the way he's always done things are suddenly vying with each other for the honor of being the way you'll both do things from now on. The first few years of marriage you get to choose which traditions and habits are going to stick and which ones are going to be tossed out along with the ugly ceramic candlesticks Great-aunt Beatrice gave you as a wedding present.

When it dawned on me, shortly after we said "I do," that my

husband's family traditions were now mine for the taking, I was eager to game the system, make this whole "merging life" thing work to my advantage, improve my life by stealing freely from his.

For example:

Rob's family had always celebrated Christmas, but all I had known growing up was that wild ride of a holiday called Hanukkah, with its eight underwhelming nights of cheap candles and crappy presents. As a kid, I'd spent December with my nose pressed up to the TV, sighing with envy as George Bailey's children decorated their tree and pressed flower petals and pulled wings off of angels (or whatever it was they did to angels—I was always a little unclear on that one).

All of which is to say: I desperately wanted a Christmas tree. But my parents refused even to consider it. We were Jewish, and Jews didn't have Christmas trees.

And then I married Rob, whose family had always celebrated Christmas. A tree was part of his tradition—and that meant it could be part of ours.

That first year we picked out a small fir and decorated it with origami birds, and the fact that the paper never caught on fire from the hot bulbs proved to me that we were meant to have a tree from then on.

There were other things I borrowed from Rob's world, some small (adults in his family played board and parlor games, something my parents never did) and some big (turns out you *are* allowed to temper truth with kindness, a total revelation to me after growing up in the Painful House of Brutal Honesty). But nothing brought home the way marriage had enriched my options as much as a ten-pound short-haired rescue cat named Lion.

To say my parents aren't into pets is like saying Hannibal Lecter's a bit of a misogynist. My dad is openly contemptuous of anyone who would willingly feed and house a dog or cat. To him, they're disruptive, dirty, demanding drains on your time and money—and, yeah, maybe they are, but so are kids, and my parents went ahead and had five of *those*.

And of course, the five of us begged for pets when we were little. That's what kids do—they ask for pets. They see *Lassie* on TV or read *Old Yeller* and decide their lives won't be complete without a faithful dear old dog to follow at their footsteps and rescue them when they fall down wells.

I was only a toddler at the time, so I have only a vague memory of the brief period of time when Mom and Dad actually succumbed to our pleas and begrudgingly agreed to get a dog. It's still hard for me to wrap my mind around the fact that they actually gave in on this one, but they were young and tired back then and our eyes were big and cute and irresistible in those days.

Not that it really matters: the dog didn't last long.

He came and went with astonishing speed, leaving nothing behind but a couple of black-and-white photos. I've been told that he bit me, but I have no memory of that. (My brother recently claimed that it was all my fault, that I tried to ride the dog like a horse, and my parents had to give him up for his own sake. I do not believe my brother. He used to cheat at Monopoly.)

After that failed experiment—and the subsequent discovery that my sisters all had pretty violent allergies to anything on four legs—my parents achieved a new level of clarity on the subject:

Scovells are not animal people. We do not have pets.

And thus it was. And thus it would ever be.

My siblings became as virulently antipet as our parents. My sisters learned to equate anything furry with itchy eyes, runny noses, blotchiness, and a general loss of sex appeal. My brother's issue was environmental: pets waste energy and resources and give nothing back.

I didn't drink the family Kool-Aid as readily as the others. For years, I remained obsessed with the idea of having a pup all my own. When I was still in elementary school, I read every novel I could find about kids who went blind and subsequently needed guide dogs. (There were more of those than you might think—it was practically a genre unto itself.) It seemed almost too easy: all you had to do was play with one illegal firework and the next thing you knew your parents were thrusting the nicest, smartest, most loyal dog at you.

I was sure I'd found the perfect solution, the one way I could get my parents to budge on the no-pets issue: they couldn't refuse their poor blinded daughter a guide dog, could they?

I thought about it a lot. Way too much. The dog was the most appealing part of the fantasy, but I was also ready to embrace the other aspects of going blind—at least as it was described in these books—like learning to tell your change by feeling the edges of the coins, having someone pin your clothing together so you always had matching outfits, and of course falling in love with the guy in your Braille class who had a deep warm voice and made devilishly funny little jokes about not being able to see.

One limiting factor: I didn't have a lot of access to defective fireworks. But I felt fairly confident I didn't need it. My eyesight was so bad that by eight, I was wearing glasses; by ten, they were as thick as Coke bottles; and by twelve, I was begging for contact lenses so I had some chance of one day being asked out on a date. Clearly I was on a myopic trajectory that would lead me right to guide-dog training camp.

To my disappointment, my vision, awful as it was, remained correctable, and I couldn't figure out any other way to convince my parents to give me a pet. As my years living at home dwindled, so did the odds that I would ever know the joys of curling up with my own little Toto.

For the next phase of my life, I was in college or moving around. Dogs weren't an option, and I forgot about wanting one. My older sisters were all getting married and settling down and having kids. None of them had pets. It never even occurred to me that they might. I assumed I'd never have a pet either. I had finally bought into the family line.

We are not animal people. I am not an animal person.

And thus it was. And thus it would ever be.

* * * * * * * *

And then I married Rob.

Leafing through his old photo albums one day after we'd joined our lives together, I noticed that page after page showed him curled up with some ball of fluff or another. Cats, mostly, but there were also a lot of photos of a silly little dachshund cruelly named Moishe. This wasn't news to me: I'd known Rob had pets growing up. I'd just never thought about it much.

But that day, something that had been dormant inside of me stirred and stretched. The little girl who had dreamed about getting a dog opened her eyes and said, "Now?"

I still wanted a dog—a sweet big loyal retriever, who would be exactly like Old Yeller except for the rabies part. And look what I'd just done—married a man who came from a family that liked dogs! Rob had had a dog! He was all over this dog thing! Our lives had just been permanently joined in matrimony. I could finally have a dog!

Rob said we couldn't get a dog.

It had something to do with his long hours and our small apartment and how it would be left at home too much and need to be walked and blahdy-blah-blah. I pretty much stopped listening at the word *no,* a tactic that's served me well through the subsequent two decades of our marriage.

But I started listening again when he said, "A cat, though . . . We could think about getting a cat."

A cat?

I didn't know how I felt about that. My exposure to cats was pretty much limited to Disney's Cinderella and various James Bond movies, so I'd always assumed they were evil. Dogs were sweet and cute and loving and threw themselves at rabid wolves for you. But cats? Cats were all claws and teeth and selfishness. They were supervillain accessories.

Still, Rob had had cats his whole childhood. And loved them. And wasn't this whole marriage thing about opening yourself up to someone else's truth? Learning to embrace something that was foreign to you because it felt right to him? Learning, in this case, to embrace a cat?

But none of my allergic sisters would be able to walk into our apartment if we got a cat. And while my parents and brother didn't have that issue, I would knowingly be laying myself open to their criticism and ridicule, since they thought it was immoral to feed a pet when kids were starving all over the world.

On the other hand, Rob's family would be fine with it.

Good enough.

We got the name of a well-regarded cat shelter. It turned out to be a single-family home that had been handed over to the felines. It didn't smell pretty. Every piece of furniture was covered by a blanket of meowing fur.

Now remember, I knew nothing about cats, except that (a) Walt Disney hated them, and (b) my sisters were allergic to them, and (c) they had many sharp parts. And now I was supposed to pick one out of the hundreds that surrounded us at this place? How do you pick out a "good" cat when they're all inherently evil?

I looked around, patted a few, and tried to pretend I wasn't afraid that they might turn on us en masse at any moment.

Even Rob was overwhelmed by the sheer numbers. "This one seems nice," he would say. "Or this one?" We petted, we scooped, we touched, we despaired.

Finally, exhausted and dispirited, I sat down and was just saying, "Maybe we should give up," when a big yellow short-haired cat suddenly jumped into my lap. He pressed his forehead against mine then started kneading my chest, purring audibly and occasionally pausing to rub his cheek against my chin.

I cut off in midwhine.

"This one," I said with a certainty I'd never known before in my life and haven't enjoyed since. "I want this one."

Keep your Old Yellers and your Shilohs and your Lassies. There has never been and there never will be a pet to rival Lion the Cat. (Okay, Lion was a stupid name, but it was still an improvement over "Puffy," which is what he'd been called up until then.)

He was terrified when we first brought him home, and hid far under the bed. I got on my knees and called to him, and he cautiously crept out and came right to me. My heart melted: he trusted me even though I didn't know the first thing about taking care of him. I took him on my lap, hugged him, and promised I'd do my best to honor that trust.

Take the best qualities of a dog—loyalty, affection, sweetness—and pair them with the best qualities of a cat—self-sufficiency, cleanliness, softness—and you had Lion. He didn't require much in the way of care: he never had a single accident, knew what a litter box was for, and used it from the moment we touched his paw to the sand. He happily ate dry food—no picky eater, he. He was always eager to jump on our laps and knead, but kept himself occupied with chasing down dust motes and attacking dangerous shoelaces when we were busy. He was my constant companion when Rob was working long hours—and Rob, a TV writer, was always working long hours during that first year of our marriage.

Oh, and one more thing? Lion was hypoallergenic. He didn't make anyone sneeze, not even my sensitive sisters.

He was the gift that kept on giving—usually dead rodents, but I appreciated them for the love tokens they were.

The floodgates were open: now that I knew the bliss of pet owner-ship, I wanted more. We adopted a tiny gray kitten. Named Ender after the hero of my favorite science-fiction novel, he proved that cats, like people, are not all equally lovable: sadly, Ender was a nut-job who'd cuddle with you for five minutes then suddenly gouge out a chunk of your arm and run off, leaving you bloody and cursing.

He did, however, enlighten me in one area: I'd never completely understood the whole "cats have nine lives" thing, but after Ender survived hanging himself from a living room curtain pull (I cut them all after that so he couldn't do it again) and after he'd taken several huge falls from heights he shouldn't have been able to reach in the first place, I realized that cats really do recover from a lot of risky business that would take any other animal down.

I never fell in love with Ender the way I did with Lion, but I tolerated his bad behavior because he was so cute (a mistake I've begged my teenage daughter not to make once she starts dating). Anyway, Lion was sweet enough for both of them: he gave me faith not just in cats but in the idea of pets. He was good and faithful and kind and warm. He was love.

Lion lived with us for many years, in several different apartments and homes, but one night a friend came to visit with his dog, and Lion ran out of the house even though it was dark out. A little while later, I heard the sound of an animal screaming. Once.

He never came home again. I had heard stories of cats that disappeared for long periods of time and then miraculously showed up on their owners' doorsteps, and for months—even years—I clung to the hope that Lion would one day reappear, come strutting up with a throaty meow just as I left the house one day. Except . . . I couldn't forget that scream. It haunted me. I knew what had happened. I could keep hoping I was wrong. But I knew.

Some coyote had attacked and eaten him, in the dark recesses of the overgrown canyon below our house.

I hope that coyote choked to death.

We haven't been petless since the day Lion came to live with us, and over the years we've branched out into other many other species. At the height of our lunacy, we had two dogs, a cat, two turtles, three mice, a frog, and three fish. (We also had four kids at that stage in our lives—I am not exaggerating when I use the word *lunacy*.) We've also had millipedes and snakes and spiders and mantids and hamsters.

And, yes, my parents have hated every single one of our pets. To this day, my father scowls at our gentle yellow Lab and tells him to "go away" if he dares to greet him at the door.

Well, what do you expect from someone who's not an animal person?

But over two decades and dozens of pets later, I still miss Lion. And when our current lazy hairball of a Persian cat (who makes my sisters sneeze their heads off) crawls on top of me and kneads my chest and purrs, I love him as much because he evokes the memory of Lion as for himself.

And I love Lion's memory not just because he was a great cat—although he was—but because of everything he meant to me in that first year of marriage.

When Rob and I adopted him together, it brought home like nothing had before that we were forging our own path together. My parents and siblings might not have been animal people, but I was part of a new family now, and that new family could be whatever Rob and I wanted it to be. It was an exhilarating realization.

And one more thing.

I had married a man who had shown me during our years of dating that he was kind and supportive. I knew I wanted to have kids with him, but I had to take on faith that he would be a good father. It's not something you can test ahead of time.

And then we got our first cat.

When Rob spoke to Lion, his voice would lower to a soft, reassuring rumble. He always had room on his lap for the cat, was always willing to give an ear scritch or endure a good, long knead—even if the claws hadn't been trimmed recently and the knead had its painful moments. If the cat was sleeping on the bed, Rob would arrange his own limbs carefully around the supine fluffy body. He never kicked or hit Lion in anger, never touched him except with affection, always was willing to clean up the occasional rat carcass or bird-bone vomit without complaint. The cat wasn't just mine; he was ours, and Rob shared the work as well as the pleasures.

Sometimes I'd look at them curled up in bed together, a man and his cat, and I knew I had linked my life with someone who would not only be a good husband but the best kind of father. Because if he could love a stupid little pet that much, if his heart was that tender and open toward an animal who had come into our lives as an adult with an unknown past, if he was willing to give up his free time to care for and protect something small and vulnerable and dependent— wasn't that evidence right there that when we actually had kids together, he would be the kindest, best father there ever was?

Yeah. It was and he is.

The First Year

CLAIRE BIDWELL SMITH

Greg and I got married on a hot July day on Cape Cod. Two months later I walked into the bathroom of our Chicago apartment and took a pregnancy test.

You're not pregnant, Greg called through the door.

When I came out of the bathroom, I handed the test to him, watching his face as he stared down at the miniature plus sign. He looked back up at me and I offered him a wobbly smile, and he returned one of his own. I was indeed pregnant.

Greg wasn't entirely convinced, though. I think this was mostly because my being pregnant didn't quite fit into his idea of what our first year of marriage was supposed to be like. It didn't exactly fit into mine either, but then again, nothing did.

Marriage and pregnancy are two things I've always felt ambivalent about. I even told Greg on our very first date that I didn't know if I ever wanted to have children. We were walking across a bridge in

Chicago's Millennium Park and it suddenly seemed like one of those things he should know about me right away.

The words trickled out of my mouth before I'd even had a chance to consider the impact they might have on my future with this man, but I needn't have worried. Greg simply smiled at me mysteriously. Either he didn't care, or he knew something I didn't.

Although that was our first official date, we'd actually known each other for a few months, having corresponded by e-mail after "meeting" when we both became writers for the same literary site. On a whim, I changed a flight, stopping in Chicago for sixteen hours so that we might finally meet in person.

I'd always scoffed a bit at the idea of love at first sight, but the moment I met Greg in baggage claim at O'Hare Airport, I knew that he was going to be my husband. I moved to Chicago three months later, and hardly a year passed before we found ourselves standing before an altar, reciting carefully written vows.

Greg is a husky-voiced and handsome writer, the son of Ohio farmers, one of six kids. When we met he'd never lived outside of the Midwest. Compared with the lengthy list of big cities I'd inhabited, coupled with my penchant for world travel and my lack of an immediate family, we were an unlikely match.

I lost both of my parents to cancer by the time I was twenty-five, and as a result, my twenties were tumultuous, and my sense of independence had become a force to be reckoned with. For me to go from living alone in Los Angeles to being married and pregnant in the space of a year was enough to make anyone dizzy.

The Monday after I took the test, Greg met me at the doctor's office to confirm the pregnancy. She gave me another test, we all peered down at another little plus sign, and then she gave us a date: June 6.

Satisfied, and also a little stunned, Greg kept his hand on my knee during the drive back to our apartment. We spent that night in a daze of wonderment. Someone was growing inside of me, part him, and part me.

That wondrous feeling never quite dissipated, although I spent most of that fall battling a morning sickness that was most prevalent in the afternoon. I would come home early from work and lie on the couch in the living room watching old TV shows. The way I felt was more akin to seasickness, and the sofa became my gently rocking boat. I thought a lot about my life during those afternoons. What I'd imagined for it, compared to what it had become.

I spent most of my twenties terribly sad and lonely, and although I knew that I didn't want to feel that way for the rest of my life, I couldn't deny that pregnancy and marriage were heavy anchors in an ocean I was used to navigating freely.

Greg was sweet those months, bringing me saltines and massaging my legs when they grew restless. His family was excited, too, although with six kids, ours would be just another number in a handful of growing grandchildren.

I missed my own mother a lot during the months that my gently swelling belly grew. There were a hundred questions I wanted to ask her, but couldn't. I listened to Greg on the phone with his own mom, happily reporting the latest update with the pregnancy, and I was envious. I could have talked to her myself, and sometimes I did, but it was never the same as I knew it would have been with my own mother. We'd had a connection that would be impossible for me to replicate with any other woman.

Perhaps this was the reason I longed for a daughter. I knew that having a girl might be my only chance to replace my long-lost mother-daughter bond. I knew that having a girl meant that in some small way I would get my mother back, if only because I would become her.

Greg and I decided not to find out the sex. Me for the already stated reasons, and Greg because he is sweet and sensitive, and would be equally at home playing with mermaids as he would with trucks. As the months wore on, we speculated constantly. Everyone around us had an opinion, too. Coworkers, checkout clerks, strangers on the street—all stopped what they were doing in order to declare their prediction. It was unanimous: I was going to have a boy.

Greg felt the baby move for the first time one cold January morning. It was early and we were lying in bed in the dark. I took his hand, pressing it to my lower abdomen at the exact moment that our unborn child gave a swift kick. Greg's eyes flew open in the dimly lit room, barreling into mine. It was one of the most intimate moments of my life.

It's one thing to commit yourself to spending the rest of your life with someone. It's another thing to create a physical manifestation of that commitment, one that's going to grow up and go to school and need new shoes and kiss someone for the first time.

As the months drew themselves out, we both grew a little wistful. Pregnancy didn't suit me. I was huge and listless, prone to hormone-induced anxiety and tearful days. I could tell that Greg missed the vibrant and happy young woman he had married only months earlier. Sometimes we whispered secrets to each other in bed, in the dark.

I wish we'd had more time to just have fun, he said into his pillow one night.

Me, too, I admitted, lying on my side to accommodate my protruding belly.

I'm afraid that I won't be a good mom, I told him. That I won't love the baby.

I'm afraid that I won't be able to support all of us. I want our baby to have a good life, he whispered back.

There was nothing either of us could say that would reassure the other. Because the truth was that we didn't have the answers. While our secrets stayed safe, hidden in the hushed gloom of our bedroom, I caught glints of them now and then in Greg's eyes or in mine, reflected back in the mirror as I observed myself.

When spring came we took a weekend and turned the guest room into a nursery. We painted the walls a pale yellow, assembled the crib, and hung a pair of soft, pretty curtains. I washed and folded dozens of little onesies and carefully folded them into the dresser.

I took a bath almost every night, and as I lay still in the clear, warm water, I tried to imagine the person growing inside me. I thought about how even though Greg and I chose each other, the baby wouldn't have the same experience—we would simply always be its parents. Greg and I—once two strangers, who are still getting to know each other—would never be anything but the two people who most understand this little person we would soon meet.

This thought gave me a sense of peace. Almost just as suddenly as I'd lost the threesome I'd always been a part of, I'd re-created it.

I went into labor on an unseasonably cool June night, four days past my due date. I'd worked hard throughout pregnancy to prepare for a natural birth and I wanted to labor without pain medications, aiming for as raw an experience as I could have. Greg had been a good sport, going along to HypnoBirthing workshops and interviewing doulas, even though the whole concept was a new one for him.

His willingness to participate in these trainings, to help me prepare for something he would mostly just witness, only served to further emphasize that I had married the right person. So far, everything about me, from my scattered past, to a grief that he could never quite relate to, had never fazed him. He embraced each facet of my personality with an interest and an openness that I myself couldn't even match.

When the time came, Greg drove us to the hospital in an old car he bought just after he graduated high school. Things went as planned and I was admitted to the alternative birthing suite. So there we were, not even married a year, huddled into each other on a queen-size bed, working to bring into the world a small version of the two of us. I gritted my teeth and screamed, squeezing Greg's hand as hard as I could.

A few hours went by before it was finally time to push, officially the hardest thing I have ever done. I sat with my back up against the headboard of the bed, Greg on my left, the doula on our right. The midwife knelt before me and a team of nurses assembled in the back of the room.

Greg told me later how each time the midwife instructed to me to push through a contraction, the nurses in the back of the room would all rise, expecting to receive the baby. I don't remember this because I had my eyes closed, straining with every muscle in my body to expel the creature everyone was so eager to meet. Greg explained that halfway through my pushing, the nurses would be able to tell that it wasn't going to happen during this particular contraction, and they would all sit down again while I not so blissfully pushed on. The sympathy in his eyes each time he told this story became tiny windows into his first experience of fatherhood, for that unrelenting ability to feel someone else's pain.

When I finally did reach the final push, I felt my hip bones spread apart, and the baby burst forth into being. Before I could really understand what had happened, Greg was placing her on my chest.

It's a girl, he said.

We both cried then, overcome by the enormity of it all. By the swift disappearance of our quiet union. By the way we had produced something so much bigger than either of us. And by the way that we would forever move through life, inextricably linked by a living extension of the first moment we met.

He Chose Me

SOPHIE LITTLEFIELD

Many years ago, when I met my future husband, I was barely twenty-four. Does that seem young to you? It does, now, to me—an age of impossible innocence, an age imbued with the sweet wrongheaded-ness of youth.

I seized upon him and he upon me. We were instantly inseparable. That part of the story you can imagine for yourself, if you've ever fallen hard and fast. It was intoxicating and invigorating and exhaust-ing all at once, and I will never, until the moment I die, forget the feeling of his gloved hand holding mine as we ice-skated beneath the frozen sparkle of the Chicago skyline at night.

It lasted a long, long time. Not forever. But this is not a story about the undoing. It is the story of what came first. If love is a lucky pebble tossed into a pond, spinning concentric circles out across the still waters, this is the story of the innermost circles, when it seems that the magic can radiate out forever and change everything. I was as foolish as any lover, and I forgive my former self without hesitation—with affection, warmly. How could I have known? The world is far more complicated than any of us imagine, and each passing year reveals a little more of the truth, glimpses of the game maker's odds. But in the beginning—and if you are lucky, as I was, it will be a long and splendid beginning—there is the shiny patina, the sleight-of-hand magic of Cupid and Eros, and if you are truly blessed, you will drink deeply.

. . . .

I came from a childhood marred by chaos and abrupt changes, rarely good; my adolescent years were marked by loss and anger and loneliness. I was the apple of no one's eye. I was often a burden, but on the worst days I was just . . . extraneous. Unneeded. Unnoticed. Unremarked.

Maybe that was why I loved the drama of fairy tales. Not just the Disney variety either; in our home were volumes of Grimm and equally frightening Polish and Russian anthologies, which I supplemented with folk and fairy tales from every culture represented in the public library of our small town. These stories were often violent and vengeful and passionate; people were constantly being starved and beaten and imprisoned. It was not enough merely to love; suitors had to prove themselves and earn their beloved's troth, and their trials were deliciously appalling if incomprehensible. I remember a tale in which seven handsome brothers were turned into swans by an angry witch. To regain human form, they had to convince seven beautiful maidens, sisters, to spin seven shirts of rough flax, which pierced their fingers while they spun. They bled extravagantly—and somehow, in the process, fell deeply in love with the brothers.

The fact that this seemed like a suitable allegory for a contemporary love affair should tell you how flawed was my understanding of human relationships. I longed for love but believed it was reserved for the beautiful; I did not delude myself that I had any potential in that regard. I noted bitterly that in folklore, the youngest sisters were always the most beautiful, clever, and faithful; I was an older sister. It did not escape me that gracefulness was required, though I knew that grace was and always would be beyond me. I was homely, too tall, awkward, clumsy, and while I expected to marry someday, I assumed it would be to some dull, equally forgettable lout, someone who would be every bit as disappointed with me as I would be with him.

. . . .

By the time I went off to college, I'd put aside fairy tales in favor of highbrow literature, the sort in which the everyday lives of unexceptional people are elevated by their fleeting rejection of the banal. I'd also grown tired of wallflowerism, and—dizzy with the possibilities presented by living where no one knew me—I managed a handy self-renovation. Those were the eighties, so it involved a lot of blue eyeliner and voluminous hair. By all external accounts it was successful; I ended up with more than enough male attention. But no matter how ardent my admirers, they never were able to assuage my essential loneliness: if they really knew me, I reasoned—the me beneath the lip gloss and the Hang Ten short shorts—they'd realize how truly unlovely I still was.

And then—only a few months into my first real job—I met him. He wasn't like the others. (Join me now, you who had your own brave passion; this is a chorus you know the words to.) My friends were surprised: we were so unsuited for each other. He didn't care what they thought, and soon I didn't care what they thought.

He was staid, dependable; he was a keeper of promises; I was all passionate longing and scattershot affection. We reached for each other with something like desperation and certainly with relief; we sensed in each other salve for what was broken in ourselves. We seized and held on tight, from the start. After our first evening together, we were never apart unless circumstances forced a separation. Mondays meant that one of us was always awake hours before dawn to get to an airport, and Fridays were sweet with the promise of being together again. That it wouldn't be forever was inconceivable. We got engaged. We got married.

As a love story, ours was nothing unusual. You probably have your own, if you chose your partner with any care at all. Early love is about seeing yourself in the other's eyes, and seeing reflected back a version of yourself that fixes your hurt places or completes what's missing. Perhaps you were an obedient child, but your lover cherishes your occasional stubbornness, your minor rebellions. Or the clumsy one can't believe her luck when her lover identifies a kind of grace no one ever noticed before, the way she ties her shoe, perhaps, or the way her bracelets jingle. "We don't love anyone," someone once told me. "We only love the self we see reflected back." This seems too cynical, even for me, even now: it is the us that is intoxicating. He gets me. She understands me. Together, we can handle anything. Together, we are more than the sum of our selves.

The twenties seem a gentle decade when viewed from middle age. Everything is rife with possibility—it hardly matters if you're broke if you use your last few dollars to buy an orchid for a lover, a length of riotous Marimekko fabric, a bittersweet confection. Later you will learn detachment and accustom yourself to the taste of disappointment. Love may crumple and fade, but you'll have things, lots of lovely things, and people will envy you, and that will be a kind of recompense.

. . . .

But for now, let's return to the home of the newly wed.

I was well suited for traditional wifery. My proudest early accomplishments were sewing a straight seam, baking a flaky biscuit, coaxing paperwhites to bloom in winter. My repertoire included unwavering topstitching, uniformly chopped carrots and potatoes, neatly braided hair, boiled icing, ruby radishes pulled from well-turned earth. The women of my family cleaved to a precise ideal of femininity: a rosary, an A-line coat, a single tube of lipstick, a bottle of perfume that would last five years of special occasions, neat unpolished nails, folded hands at church, and one ankle turned just so in front of the other when posing for photographs—these were the hallmarks of womanhood that I observed and absorbed.

I brought these notions into my marriage with far, far more conviction than I would have ever admitted to—but I also longed to be elegant. Our friends were sophisticated; they had nice taste, expensive things, and I coveted not just their clothes and sunglasses and silver frames and good dishes, but their entire pasts. Debutante balls, boarding schools, inherited jewelry—it was the fashion then, and probably still is, to affect a mild contempt for all of these if you possessed them, indifference if you did not. After all, the hard work of inventing oneself involves a certain amount of casting off, no matter what you bring from your past.

Still, my life seemed so humble by comparison. Our friends—my husband's friends, whom I claimed for my own, hungrily, longing for acceptance—called me "FMA." That acronym stands for Fucking Miss America, and I know they coined it with affection—I was the one among us that made every dish from scratch, sewed my own black-tie gowns, filled our balcony with pots of flowers. But I was ashamed of my nickname, too. I wanted to be like them, not different. I wanted a long-standing manicure appointment and a stack of take-out menus and a horrendous dry-cleaning bill.

There was one place, however, where being FMA felt right, and that was in my marriage. I wanted to be a good wife. I wanted to be a helpmate. That term—outdated even then—was irresistible to me, because it suggested I would be needed. That I would complete my husband as he would complete me. I wanted my husband to shine, and I would be content to stand in his shadow. I wanted to be the wind beneath his wings, and even as I cringe at how hackneyed that phrase has become, I remember how I turned it in my mind over two decades ago and thought, *Yes, yes, that's right.* I would hang his shirts in the closet. (That image is so powerful, in fact, that it made its way into a short story I wrote a while back, and is perhaps the perfect still shot of marriage for me—a wife, alone during the day, hanging her husband's shirts with care, with affection. Their fabric is fragrant from the laundry and she smoothes the fabric with her hand, straightening the shoulders on the hanger, imagines her husband dressing for work, finding the perfectly pressed shirt pleasing.)

Other couples brought store cakes to potlucks; I baked. I made curtains for our apartment. Together, my husband and I planted the flower beds behind our building with impatiens; the smell of the turned earth on that long-ago May morning may be the sweetest memory of that year. The sun was warm on our backs and we laughed at the dirt ground into our knees; later I would shower off the grime and sweat and change into a summer-sheer dress, and we would drink wine on our balcony, and we were so blessed, so blessed. I was smug, and I know now that conceit is a sin that fate punishes with glee; fate waits with the patience of the inevitable. Still, I pitied those other wives, the ones who didn't know how to sew a hem and had to send their husband's pants out, the ones who would correct their husbands in conversation or laugh too loud . . . who did not understand the blessing they'd been given, even though it was right in front of their faces.

Threaded throughout all of this first year of marriage was the stunning amazement that I had been chosen. "I am a wife," I whispered to myself the day after our wedding, folding the dress I had made, mindful of the thousands of tiny pearls and sequins I sewed on by hand. I could imagine no greater honor.

Cards and invitations arrived, addressed to Mr. and Mrs. Robert Littlefield. I didn't mind the disappearance of my former self. That self had not served me well, I thought. When I had to check a box on a subscription form, choosing "Ms." or "Mrs.," I chose the latter with great satisfaction.

I took my place at my husband's side and I cherished it. I remember moments with great clarity. My ex-husband remembers every phone number, every address we ever had; he can tell you where we went each summer and whom we saw. These details don't last for me, but I remember how he looked in the Brooks Brothers shirt I picked to bring out the color of his eyes. I remember the brass dish where he used to leave his keys when he came to the door—and the smell of the polish I used on it. I remember the gifts he gave me, and I still have them, wrapped with care and tucked into the bottoms of boxes, underneath out-of-season coats and the children's sports trophies. There was a picture frame, the green of malachite. An earring, a gold-tone crystal-studded hoop, its mate lost long ago.

I wanted children right away. I would have been happy to start trying on our honeymoon. There would be four, all girls; when their father came home from work, their hair would be combed neatly and they would have made things for him, leaves pressed between waxed paper and cookies decorated with colored sugar, and they would be pretty like me and he would call us "his girls."

On our first anniversary we thawed the frozen bit of wedding cake and took it outside on the sunny porch. It was dry, almost inedible. We laughed and drank champagne instead. He opened the bottle with a flourish; I did the dishes when we were finished. We had our roles and we relished them. I thought they would see us through.

Lying to myself lost its appeal somewhere north of forty. The denial that served me so well as a layer of protection—like the cartilage around a knuckle or the WD-40 on a hinge—sloughed away, and I was left with an acuity that proved impossible to cast off.

Here was the long-evaded truth: cherished ideals and best intentions were not, in the end, enough. And so, with great sadness and regret, we parted.

When I look back at my young marriage, I was so full of hopes, so eager to quit the loneliness of my past and become not just someone new, but part of something even further removed from who I was before: part of a couple. But I think that even then I knew the old self would not stay buried forever. Was it a mistake to keep it in the box, sealed and shoved back on the shelf, left to simmer and churn until the day it would come back to claim its place?

I'm not sure I think it was. There was joy in that year, genuine can't-believe-my-luck glory at finding myself by his side.

He chose me, I think still. That, at least, will always be true.

The Marry Boy

JOSHILYN JACKSON

My marriage can drive. That's what I said to Scott on our last anniversary. Sixteen years since we stood up in the chapel at Fort Something on a date neither of us can ever remember and made all kinds of promises. I don't specifically remember those either. Obey wasn't one of them, I know that.

The rest is washed away in a whirling vortex of taffeta and organ music, a buffet with a shrimp tree and way too much champagne.

I was going to grad school, living in the middle of downtown Chicago, and Scott was living an hour away, having just finished his MFA. We wanted to be married in our southern hometown, so my mother, the Once and Future Belle, planned the wedding for us. I told her she could do whatever she wanted as long as (1) it wasn't pink, and (2) at the end of the day, I was married to Scott. I came home between semesters to find my happy mommy planning the swirliest pink wedding in the history of time. When I reminded her of my terms, she gave me the Belle-eye and said, with zero irony, "It isn't pink. It's 'seashell.'"

By the time the day ended, I was married to Scott, so I decided to call it a win. We honeymooned in New Orleans and moved to Oak Park, and he got a job and I got a master's degree. We had an excellent boy child and Scott found a weird career niche and flourished and moved me back to the South, where I belong. I wrote a novel, and we had another baby, and then I wrote more novels and he got some promotions and we gathered up hordes of feckless pets to chew up and ruin all our furniture, days piling on days, until now our marriage can drive. In another year and change, it will be able to vote, and soon after that, we can legally take our marriage out drinking. I'm looking forward to that. Twenty-one, the Vodka Anniversary.

Yesterday, I asked Scott, "Tell me about the first year we were married."

He was quiet for a moment, brows together, and then he said, "Oh! Our apartment had that god-awful galley kitchen."

"What else?" I said.

After another silent minute, he shrugged. "I got nothin'."

That would have been plenty damning, if I hadn't been asking him because I'd drawn a complete blank, too. I hadn't even been able to conjure up the galley kitchen.

I was asking because one of the two babies we had, the girl one, the youngest, came out of the womb a full-on Belle. It must skip a generation, because I was born a barn rat. Now in my forties, I still don't know how to blow-dry my hair and I can never remember to apply accessories. But the day we finally brought Maisy Jane home from the hospital? She peered about with her bleary baby eyes, seeking a bracelet that would complement her receiving blanket without being too matchy-matchy.

Because she is a Belle, one of the mystifying-to-me topics that consumes Maisy Jane is her wedding. More than that—her marriage. It began when she was barely three. That's when she started asking me who her "Marry Boy" would be. At first she thought the Marry Boy should be her daddy. I agreed that he was excellent husband material, but alas, he was already taken. Next she picked my father, but he is righteously preclaimed by the Once and Future Belle. After I ruled out Uncle Bobby and Daniel, her tallest, most handsome cousin, she deigned to settle for her brother, Sam. He, a lordly third grader, had zero interest in marrying little sisters and turned her down flat.

I told her she hadn't yet met her Marry Boy (probably). When she did, he would not (Lord willing) be any kind of a relation, but a new fellow, and that was how our family would grow. I was relieved to see she stopped trying to get into a contractual engagement with a close blood relative, but she immediately started casting about for her Marry Boy in the world around her.

She met her first potential Marry Boy in preschool. She came home all dreamy, talking about this three-year-old lothario who went by the overly virile name of Colby. I had to forcibly restrain my husband from going out and shooting a toddler, assuring him that Colby was oblivious to Maisy Jane's ambitions for him. Colby was more interested in *Blue's Clues*, quite frankly.

Maisy Jane is eight now, and she has remained vigilant, always on the lookout. Currently, she isn't sure if her Marry Boy will be Justin at school or Kyle at church. She likes to lie on my bed on her stomach and swing her feet back and forth in the air and muse about their relative merits. Terrifying, how rigorous my girl child is in her Marry Boy investigations.

She has asked me endless questions about when I met her dad (I was nineteen, he was twenty), how I knew he was the one (I didn't. He knew, right away, but I was clueless for seven years), and what our wedding was like (I dragged out the photo album and let her look at a young me swathed in a pouf of satin with multiple petticoats and a cathedral train, surrounded by seven swirly, be-pinked bridesmaids).

We recently went to a young friend's wedding, and now Maisy Jane is fascinated by what will happen to the bride next. She wants to know what it's like to be a "Newlyweed," as she calls it.

I am drawing a terrifying blank. I think it was probably fun. It must have been an adventure. But it's not all that clear or distinct from the other fifteen. The year that stands out to me is the bad year, somewhere in the middle, when Maisy Jane was born too early, and we weren't sure if we would get to keep her. That year? Oh, hell yes, I remember that one. But the first is only a year, buried under and hard to distinguish from every other year I have spent with her father.

I told her we had a crappy galley kitchen, but that wasn't what she wanted.

So I've been trying to remember. We had a lot less of everything. Less children, certainly, and that means less responsibility. We had less security, but less need for it as well. Less money. A lot less, as I was in school and Scott had just hit the job market with seven years of higher education in theater.

The only thing we had more of back then was probably sex, which is not something I want to explain to my third grader. I have only recently told her, using a matter-of-fact tone and scientifically accurate terms, the process for making babies. She listened earnestly, then made a disapproving mouth and asked, "Do you have to actually touch the boy for it work?" When I told her that yes, the touch part was mandatory, she declared that she and Marry Boy would be adopting.

I also remember when Scott made the transition from friend to Marry Boy. I met him when we both had summer acting jobs at a regional repertory theater. He was a tall, dark-haired boy who reminded me of an adolescent German shepherd: innocent-eyed, with long skinny legs and feet way too big for his body. I was always in the middle of everything, usually instigating crime, and he stood on the edge of the action, observing and cataloging. He barely ever spoke. I liked that about him, as I never stopped speaking. I parked myself near him and gabbled at him for a couple of hours.

Instead of letting my endless flow of words wash over him and away, he seemed to be actually listening. I got addicted to it. After a few weeks, I got a bug up my butt about making him talk back. I felt that he knew everything about me, while he remained a silent cipher. I started questioning him relentlessly, trying for answers that were longer than five words, trying to learn him.

Back in those days, I never would have dated a boy like him. He was much too nice to me; I liked my romantic entanglements to be rife with intrigue and melodrama. And yet, no matter who I was dating, his opinion was always the one that mattered most in my head. He shaped the person I grew up to be, and I shaped him, too. I would meet his girlfriends, and I would be nice to them, because in some deep inside part, I understood that they weren't terribly relevant. None of them mattered to him the way I did.

It was only when he got serious about one particular girl that I realized I could lose him. We were both home at Christmas, and he told me he was ring-shopping and thinking about Valentine's Day.

"He's going to marry her! It's disgusting," I raged to my mother. "Do you think that it will wreck our friendship?"

"Oh yes," the Once and Future Belle said wisely. "Absolutely. Smart women don't let their husbands have girls for best friends."

"Well, he can't marry her, then," I said.

My mother wisely kept her counsel to herself. She didn't want to spook me off of him via maternal approval. Belles can smell a potential Marry Boy from miles off; Scott had long been her dark-horse pick for me.

All she said was, "Men like Scott get snapped up fast. He's going to marry someone."

Then she left me to fume and stomp and relook at this boy I had known for years now. For the first time, I noticed that the German-shepherd puppy had grown into his big feet. Scott had become a hell of a man, but I'd been too close to him to notice him changing.

At that time Scott was living in Chicago, and I was living in Atlanta. After Christmas we both went home, and that might have ended it, had we both not been drawn back a couple of weeks later. I'd come to be a bridesmaid in a friend's wedding. He was home to bury his father.

After the reception, I went to check on him. It was late. His mother and sister had gone to bed, so I drove him to my parents' house. We sat in my backyard, in a teeny wooden structure surrounded by azalea and gardenia bushes. My mother called it "the gazebo, where you can entertain a beau." I called it "the Hut," and it was used exclusively as a place to sneak off to and smoke.

We talked all night. In the starless hour right before dawn, he said, "I want to order a Domino's pizza. I want the delivery guy to take more than thirty minutes, and then I want to punch him in the face. I need to be angry. I want to be angry with my dad for smoking, and for getting lung cancer. He's dead, though. I can't be angry with him, so I want to be furious with someone."

I put out my cigarette, ashamed of it, and said, "I can make you angry."

He laughed. "You've been my best friend for almost seven years now, Jackson, and you have yet to make me angry. Please. Bring it."

I took a deep breath. "I don't want you to marry that girl. I lied when I said I liked her." That was all I had planned to say, but my mouth kept talking. "In fact, you are not allowed to marry her. You are only allowed to marry me."

He looked at me, calm and carefully observing, the way he always was, and then he shrugged. "I've been waiting for you to say that for seven years."

And that was it. We sat there, both of us scared and dumbfounded, but with the brightest kind of happiness building unstoppably up behind that.

I said, "Well. We should probably kiss."

So we did. It was a good kiss. A really good kiss. Maybe not worth seven years of waiting—and Lord knows it should have happened earlier—but it came pretty damn close. The air had that crisp apple edge it sometimes gets in mild, southern winters. To this day, when the seasons change and the air gets crisp, I find myself breathing deep, and that familiar bright happiness still rises in me.

Then we separated and stared at each other, and that was far as it went. We were both in relationships, and we didn't want to start with each other wrong, by cheating other people. I told him to call me in three days. If he was free, I said. If he had meant it. I told him I was pretty much in love with him and would be single come tomorrow, regardless.

Before we parted, I made it clear that I wasn't interested in "trying it out" or "seeing if this would work." I wouldn't risk losing his friendship for the sake of some dumb experiment. Either he was all in, total commitment, heading toward marriage with a bullet, or we would simply go home, give it a few days to settle, chalk it up to 4 a.m. lunacy after the emotional tumult of a wedding and a funeral. We could, I said, return to our friendship relatively unscathed.

Three days later, the phone rang. He had picked to go all in.

I do remember, quite specifically, a few things that happened in the months after that. It is an odd transition, to see one's best friend's head perched atop of the lovely, naked male body one has just ridden to mad pleasure. But this is not information I particularly wish to share with my eight-year-old. Also, strictly speaking (and here we must ask the Once and Future Belle to delicately avert her eyes), that transition may have happened slightly before the first year of my marriage technically began.

So now Maisy Jane pesters for stories of Newlyweedhood, and I have nothing for her but an anecdotally barren sense of general happiness. She blinks her round blue eyes at me, dissatisfied, but this is all I have to say to her:

I hope you don't remember your first year of marriage either. I hope you marry your best friend and stay his best friend. You will have more fun with him than anyone. You will always be on his side, and he will always be on yours. Even when you are fighting with each other, you will always have each other's back. You'll be able to tell him anything, even though his opinion matters most, because you know he won't judge you. He will look at you like you invented pretty, and he will always, always be so nice to you. Pick a Marry Boy like that.

Because that is what being married to your father has been like.

That's what you see us living together, every day, when he makes the perfect coffee, even though he doesn't drink it, and I leave Yes playing on the radio even though that squawky guitar noise gets on my last nerve.

When your own daughter comes to you to ask about Marry Boys, when she asks you how the first year of your marriage went, I hope that all you can say is that maybe you had a crappy galley kitchen, but otherwise, it was good. So good, you can't remember it as a separate thing. It will just be one of many years with him, blended into a long string of time that you think of as the best years of your life.

WE WILL CARVE OUT A FUTURE

The Devil's Playground

REBECCA RASMUSSEN

Brides scare me. So do cakes that are as tall as me and cost more than my first car. Don't get me started about billowy white dresses that make people weep into handkerchiefs one day and then end up hanging for time immemorial in the back of closets the next. There. I said it. I'm cynical about weddings when people in the world go daily without nourishing food, clean water, and sturdy roofs over their heads. How much does the average wedding cost? Five thousand? Ten thousand? Twenty? Any of those figures is an awfully high price to pay for ceremony, and yet I am a married woman and was, technically, a bride in 2006.

I didn't grow up dreaming of becoming a bride, as you may have guessed. I grew up sticking my feet in the muddy creek behind my father's farm in Wisconsin. I played with barn cats. I swam. I caught fish. I even read a few books in the hammock while my brother taunted me with branches from pricker bushes. I was a tomboy, and if you must know the truth, when I was three, I refused to be a flower girl in my father and stepmother's winter wedding because apparently, to me, the dress looked like curtains.

Though it seems I wasn't destined to be a winter bride, or a bride at all, for that matter, over the years I did dream plenty about falling in love with a smart and kind man who happened to wear a tweed sport coat. I dreamed about all of the books we would read together, all of the creeks we would tromp through, and all of the calamine lotion and cotton balls we would use up. I dreamed of the adventures we would have.

And it turns out that at the age of twenty, that's exactly what happened to me in Fort Collins, Colorado—sans the sport coat. I met my future husband, who was framing houses at the time, while I was finishing up an undergraduate degree in English. I loved to bring him lunch at the job site and watch two-by-fours turn into houses where dinners would be made, kids would grow up, and people would grow old. I loved the fine layer of sawdust on his skin. I loved that this fellow wore Carhartt by day and reading glasses by night.

I loved him.

After I graduated, my future husband and I moved to Pennsylvania so I could continue my studies in fiction writing. After that, we moved to Massachusetts so he could finish a degree in classics he'd started in Colorado. His knees and back had taken a beating over the years, framing lives for other people. And though it was a difficult job to let go of, my future husband decided it was time to frame his own life. At that point we had been together for five years, had lived together for three, and had been sharing our finances for one. We'd merged, so to speak. And we were trucking along just fine.

And then, four months after my twenty-seventh birthday, at

spring's first touch, I found out I was pregnant. Even though we didn't know what we were going to do, we knew what we were going to do. Our combined fifty-four years of experience navigating this earth told us were going to have that baby. A girl, it would turn out. With tiny bubble-gum toes.

"And we have to get married," my future husband said.

"Excuse me?" I said.

"You, me, married."

I'm not going to lie to you: it took some convincing. It turns out that *bride* wasn't the only word that scared me. I grew up under the auspices of D-I-V-O-R-C-E and so did my future husband. Both of us shuttled back and forth between families when we were kids. Both of us endured parents who didn't get along. In my future husband's case: at all. So it was odd to me that tradition would take hold of him so firmly. That he thought it was not only something we should do, but also that we must do for each other and for our future child. M-A-R-R-I-A-G-E. Not only did he propose it, but he also proposed that we throw some wedding rings into the mix.

Dear Lord, I thought.

"Really?" I said.

I know now that this is not a "normal" response to the offer of shiny (in my case vintage) jewelry. Most of my friends tell wonderful stories of their husbands kneeling down and professing their love, sometimes in private, sometimes in public, always in a completely endearing way. As much as I have connected with their stories, I didn't grow up wanting this to be mine. But I didn't grow up wanting to be a naysayer either.

"We're not our parents," my future husband said.

So off we went to the beautiful hill town of Brattleboro, Vermont, to buy some rings. On that cool spring day, our exhaust system fell off twenty miles south of Brattleboro.

"Maybe it's a sign," I said while we stood on the side of the highway.

"Maybe it's just an old car," my future husband said.

But I saw a trace of doubt appear along with the lines in his forehead from working too many summers outside without wearing sunscreen, and it worried me. That day my future husband secured what he could with tethers and we ended up making it to Brattleboro and choosing a too-large titanium ring for him and an occlusion-filled half-carat recycled diamond for me. This marked the beginning of an ill-fated period my husband and I now call "What Else Can Go Wrong?" that included an ultrasound that scared us deeply, a dwindling savings account, a tuition bill we didn't know how we were going to pay, and a bout of all-day, sixteen-week morning sickness that nearly killed us both.

Which brings me to our June wedding that year. Since we decided to get married so quickly, unfortunately our families couldn't make the trip across the country for the event. By then I was about four months pregnant, just over the worst of the morning sickness and the stuffing-myself-with-feathery-white-bread phase, and I was starting to look the part of soon-to-be mother. Things were looking up, and out.

My soon-to-be husband asked if he could wear a pair of high-top Converse to the ceremony and I said yes, which made him smile my favorite of his smiles: his boyish one. I bought a simple little sundress at Target and a pair of sandals. That morning, we took pictures of each other on our leaning second-floor porch, me in front of a spider plant and him in front of an old attic table I'd made a craft project out of.

Although we're not together in the photographs, we look sweet and young and happy. These photographs are even dearer to me than the ones the justice of the peace took of us in our backyard later that morning.

"I've never seen a bride wear black before," the justice said when she arrived, and to be honest, it didn't occur to me that I was wearing black on my wedding day and that symbolically black was a little odd. I bought it because it had cute crisscrossing straps and was one of the few dresses that shielded my stomach from judgment and me from the time-immemorial-in-the-closet thing. And also because it was one we could afford.

"You look pretty," my almost husband assured me.

"Do you have vows prepared?" the justice said.

"We were planning on saying 'I do,'" I said, smiling at my Converse-clad darling.

"Absolutely not," the justice said, and proceeded to pull out rumpled sheets of paper from her purse. "You can read these."

Oh dear, we thought, but did as we were told, even though the writer in me said *blech!* internally the whole time. I promise to love you when the lilies are in bloom. I promise to love you when the petals wilt and brown and fall to the ground . . .

Why? Why? Why? We were in Emily Dickinson country, for heaven's sake!

When we were finally alone again, my husband and I hugged each other in our backyard for a long time, laughing and smiling. We'd survived the blooming lilies and the browning ones, too. And we were married. And we loved each other. And we had a lovely little girl on the way.

My husband touched my stomach, and I touched it, too.

Our rings glinted in the sunlight.

After a while we threw our bags in the car, stopped for bagels at our favorite breakfast joint, and were off to a place we would come to think of as the Devil's Playground, although we thought of it as Connecticut then. Our very good friends Jack and Mara were getting married and my husband was supposed to play the banjo with a bluegrass band during the ceremony. Mara is a very traditional woman who had been dreaming of her wedding since she was a little girl, so we decided we weren't going to tell her and Jack about our bizarro-world version of a wedding. We weren't going to rain on her pretty white tent that would end up holding platters of lobster tails with drawn butter and over two hundred well-dressed people from all over the East Coast.

It turns out we would barely make it to that tent, and here's why: after two hours of driving, we pulled up to the World's Worst Motel.

There were only two motels in the area, according to Mara's wedding invitation, and we knew upon first glance why the other one was booked months in advance. This was either a motel where we would get sliced up à la *Psycho* or eaten up c/o les roaches. We weren't even thinking about bedbugs then. We were wondering (a) how we would stay there for two nights, and (b) how a place like this could cost $120 a night. A man whom I'll call Al for the duration of the essay came out of the office with a cigarette in one hand and a doorknob in the other to show us to our room.

"Is that our doorknob?" I said.

"Yes," Al said.

In the future, if I ever walk up to a motel room without a doorknob, I'll know to walk back to my car straightaway and drive to the nearest campground, which means I'll also know to pack a few sleeping bags and a tent in the trunk just in case for situations like this.

We'd booked a nonsmoking room, but since Al walked into the room smoking and the walls were a greasy yellow, that distinction was not meant to be. Once Al put the doorknob in the door, he took our credit card and left us to explore our room.

"Is it as bad as I think it is?" I said.

"Worse," my husband said.

Not only was everything a smoky yellow, the bedding was clearly soiled from someone else's bodily fluids, the half-torn, once-white carpet had what looked like bloodstains on it, and the fan in the corner was covered with dark gray dust several inches thick. Forget about the promise of air-conditioning or a window screen, this room was the filthiest my husband and I had ever been in. And the smell! My God, the smell. A cross between BBO (Beyond BO, from our favorite *Seinfeld* episode) and old meat.

Before we could either cry or revolt or run, our friends, who didn't know about our earlier vows, appeared in the doorway.

"Oh God, yours is completely horrific, too," they said. "We thought we might be able to bunk up with you."

"Maybe we should all just sleep in the car," I said.

"Maybe it's one of those things that gets better the more you drink," my husband said, and the other husband agreed.

The other wife—who was also pregnant—scowled. "What are we supposed to do?"

"There's a grocery store right down the street," her husband said.

"You can get some licorice," my husband added gently, and though I had been openly craving Twizzlers, I scowled, too. I might have even said, "Bite me."

But I'll tell you this: anything was better than being stuck in that room, so we went to the grocery store, which was nearly as dirty as the motel, and the husbands bought a twelve-pack of local beer and the wives bought Twizzlers and chips. This wife even snuck in a small brick of yellow cheese, too.

A few hours later, we were off to Mara's parents' house to rehearse in the woods where the wedding would take place the next morning. My husband had just struck the last banjo string and I was just sinking my teeth into a water cracker with a hunk of Brie on it when he said three very fateful words to me: Where's the bathroom?

Thus began the worst four days of our lives, though we didn't know it yet.

"What's wrong?" I said.

Can't talk. Must run.

"What?"

Oh God, Rebecca.

After I stood outside the bathroom door for over half an hour, trying to look nonchalant while people passed by with plates of gourmet food and prettily colored cocktails, my husband emerged, his face pale as chalk, his hands shaking.

"I think I have food poisoning," he said. "You have to take me home."

"I'll get the keys," I said, slightly more cheerily than was appropriate.

Home. What a wondrous word! I was already picturing our cozy and clean bed, the smell of fresh lilacs from the bouquet on the kitchen counter, the view of the magnolia tree from our living room window.

"Are you going to make it in the car?" I said, thinking of the winding country roads out of Connecticut and back to Massachusetts.

"It's only a few minutes to the motel. I'll stick my head out the window."

Poof! Gone were my dreams of fresh flowers and clean linens.

"We have to hurry," my husband said.

. . . .

I would like to be able to tell you that the fresh air did my husband good and that we were able to turn around and go back to the rehearsal party, that we sat all night beneath the stars with everyone else and played music and enjoyed the lovely summer evening.

But we didn't.

My husband spent our wedding night slung around the commode like a collar, with me sitting on the other side of the door with a decade-old phone book because he didn't want me and the baby to get sick if what he had wasn't food poisoning.

The nearest hospital was twenty miles away, and for several hours my husband was on the verge of letting me take him there.

The room now smelled more of vomit than meat.

Near midnight, when there was nothing left for my husband to expel, he crawled into the dirty old bed and fell asleep. I sat in the stained chair beside the bed for a while, eating Twizzlers and watching the one channel that came in on the dusty TV.

That night I learned about the history of soap and soap production, and I was glad for all the images of cleanliness and health the white bubbles conjured. I looked over at my husband, who was curled up like a child in the bed, the dirty blanket tucked under his chin.

At half past two, I turned off the TV.

Why did we have to be so different from everyone else? I thought. *Maybe if we'd had a normal wedding and a normal honeymoon, this wouldn't be happening to us.*

I wondered if this was what our future looked like. Smelled like.

My wedding ring didn't glint in this light.

Just before I crawled into bed next to him, I looked out the window. Across the street, lighted by a single country streetlamp, was a sign that said, *Welcome to the Devil's Playground, day passes $5.*

⁕ ⁕ ⁕ ⁕ ⁕ ⁕

We woke the next morning to sunshine and birdsong, to a magical reprieve from the illness—a potent flu bug, it turns out—that would strike our growing baby and me the moment we set foot back in our home in Massachusetts. Both of us had welts up and down our legs from the then-apparent infestation of bedbugs in the mattress, but we smiled at each other. It was our first morning as husband and wife, and after a night like the previous one, that meant something to both of us.

We had weathered our first storm, and we were all right.

All of the fears we shared and didn't share about marriage seemed to dissipate while we lay in that bed together, occasionally scratching our welts, wishing for a bulk-size bottle of calamine lotion, and eating stale Twizzlers. Despite a botched trip to get rings, a wedding with lilac vows, and a bout of violent illness, we were still us.

During our first year together and all the years thereafter, we've never given that up, which is the main reason I believe we have a successful marriage. It's how we've been able to endure (often outendure) bitter arguments, financial hardships, and great loss. Other people we know love each other; we love us, and it's made all the difference.

Later that day, my husband played the banjo beautifully, and our friends were married beneath a bright June sun. I piled my plate with lobster tails and prime rib, and we danced under a strand of paper lanterns late into the night. It was lovely.

Did we deserve all that trouble for monkeying with tradition? Some people would say yes. Some would say no. Would we have stayed at the charming motel up the road if we could have? Absolutely.

But it's the Devil's Playground that we took pictures of before we drove home: a nature park complete with a creek and fish and mud.

That morning, we paid our five dollars and walked along the gravel drive to the water. My husband took a picture of me, and I took one of him.

In them, we look ragged but happy. We look like us.

Just before we put the camera away and dipped our toes into the murky water, we hesitated on the bank of the creek for the slightest moment.

"Do you think it's cold?" I said.

"Refreshing," my husband said.

I smiled. My husband reached for my hand. All at once we sprang forward.

The Last Honeymoon

SUSAN SHAPIRO

Since Aaron wasn't into travel adventures, I planned our first vacation as husband and wife myself, expecting Jamaica to be as romantic and exotic as I remembered. Unfortunately everything went wrong from the moment we landed. As we toted huge duffel bags I'd overpacked through slow-moving customs, a tall, skinny blonde ran up to hug my new husband. Laura was his best pal's old girlfriend. What a coincidence—she was also honeymooning here! Ignoring her new bald spouse, she glommed onto Aaron, asking him about his ex-fiancée (they used to double-date). This taller, thinner, younger, lighter female from Aaron's past reminded me that at thirty-five, I was no longer a babe. Especially in ninety-five-degree heat after a four-hour flight into this rickety foreign airport.

In the cab to our hotel, I scanned Ocho Rios, which the travel agent had suggested. It was filled with fancy hotels, not my scene. You couldn't walk to a mango stand or art fair here like in the cooler city of Negril, where I'd previously stayed. I felt claustrophobically marooned at our four-star resort—where suntan lotion was twenty dollars and everything closed at 9 p.m. Our tiny room had a not-so-king-size bed, too small for a six-foot-four giant and his five-foot-seven bride. Switching to a suite on a lower floor, we were awoken at 8 a.m. with Bob Marley blaring at the pool right outside our room.

The buffet meals and luaus with roasted pigs included in the room rate felt hokey, filled with tourists my parents' age. I wanted to stick to my Atkins eating plan and exercise. But Aaron didn't want to go hiking, snorkeling, or waterskiing. He preferred to relax, read, drink banana rum punch, and indulge in meals of codfish fritters, fried sweet plantain chips, coco bread, rice bread, and Jamaican bread pudding—all taboo on my diet. I smoked more, since cigarettes were an appetite suppressant. Aaron knew I was a nicotine addict during our entire six year off-and-on courtship. But now he complained about the smell of my cigarettes. Constantly. I took to puffing away outside, at the beach.

"Come in the water with me," I begged.

"I don't swim," he said, his pale face hidden by the *New York Times*, a bunch of books under his chair.

Comparing it to my last trip here made it clear: I'd chosen the wrong groom.

* * *

"This is like a honeymoon," I'd told my boyfriend George, seven years earlier.

We were lying on the white sand during our ten picturesque days on the cliffs of Jamaica in a ten-dollar-a-day cabin with no electricity he'd found. George put away my books, took me snorkeling and waterskiing, and taught me to swim the butterfly. We were twenty-eight-year-old Greenwich Village rebels obsessed with art (I was a poet; he was into theater), escaping our day jobs. George was a tan, lean, athletic globe-trotter with dark hair and thick glasses, a Jewish Clark Kent. He made me feel younger, lighter, casually chic, like a Ralph Lauren magazine spread. Our last night in Negril we drank Red Stripe, smoked ganja on the beach. In a mock ceremony, he placed a bone ring on my finger in front of a blazing fire. Then we went skinny-dipping in the ocean. George was a torpedo in the water; I couldn't keep up with him.

Back in New York, we slept together on my gray futon, lodged on the wooden bed frame he gave me from his *Hamlet* set. Frustrated with work, he planned more exotic trips. I had bigger Manhattan ambitions and urged him to do theater rather than just teach at the Brooklyn college close to where he grew up. I hooked him up with producers from the Kitchen and La Mama. All that came of it was his best compliment: "If I'd met you in high school, I would have been a Broadway director."

At literary events I'd take him to, George was shy. In bed, he was aggressive, preferring his place and the lights on. Fooling around one night, he asked why I'd shut the lamp and my eyes. I admitted that I was getting hot picturing him ravishing a female stranger.

"Then you're not really with me," he accused. "It's like you're not here."

From then on I kept my eyes open—but only literally. It turned out my fantasy was prophetic. When I learned he was sleeping with a student actress from his school play, I left him, feeling betrayed. He was still calling when a girlfriend fixed me up with Aaron, a TV writer she called "a major mensch."

Aaron was big, sweet, smart, messy, easygoing, and warm, wearing jeans, sneakers, and untucked flannel shirts—the anti-George. He reminded me of my burly brothers in the Midwest. He had a handsome face and bushy head of salt-and-pepper curls I liked running my fingers through. But he was eleven years older, four inches taller, and thirty pounds heavier than the slighter-built George, whom I was still hung up on. I wondered if, like the Joni Mitchell song, Aaron would take me like I was, "strung out on another man."

Aaron said his old girlfriend still phoned him and he wasn't ready either, no pressure, no rush to bed. Turned out he was a great kisser and bear hugger who made so many dark hilarious jokes about decapitation and serial killers I had to tell him to shut up or I couldn't concentrate on making out. He called me gorgeous; I joked that our age difference made me eleven years hotter than I was. Both fast-talking obsessive readers and newspaper addicts, we spent Saturday night lying around with four New York papers on the couch at midnight, only our feet touching. He loved my freelance paperback column, which George had barely noticed. Every weekend, Aaron took me to dinner, mentioning which book sounded fascinating. I'd keep the advance galley, giving him the hardcover copy on our next date.

I'd grown up with a Jewish doctor dad in West Bloomfield, while Aaron grew up with a Jewish judge father in Westchester. We were from the same family, we joked. Still, Aaron seemed too old, staid, slow, and conservative. He wouldn't work out with me, didn't like healthy food, traveling, or beaches. After a few months of dating, I complained that he wasn't my type.

"Your type is neurotic, self-destructive, and not interested in you. Keep seeing Aaron," said the (happily married) friend who'd set us up. So I did. Aaron was honest, loyal, and kind. But I talked, wrote, and walked fast, while he was so snail-paced, a crony had ironically nicknamed him "Flash."

When he took a television job in L.A., I realized I didn't want to lose him and jumped his bones. After several years of bicoastal dating, I asked, "What are you waiting for, Social Security?" By the time he proposed, I was thirty-five. I wanted to tie the knot in a black gown at a late-night bohemian soiree surrounded by poet and artist friends. My mother had traditional ideas for her only daughter that Aaron said we should honor. So I was married twice the summer of 1996, in two weddings with two dresses in two different cities. The black wedding was officiated by Aaron's father, the judge, in a SoHo loft. The white wedding was led by my parents' rabbi at their Michigan country club.

For our honeymoon, I chose Jamaica because it wasn't too far away or terribly expensive. I had poignant recollections of my trip there with George. Maybe subconsciously I hoped to trump those memories with a real honeymoon beside a faithful guy who'd given me a real ring and commitment. Alas, my honeymoon with Aaron seemed like a bad sitcom and left me with more doubts.

There was room for the new seashells I'd gathered in the hand-made box I'd bought last time. But for the first year of our union, nothing else fit. Aaron and I argued about his messiness, his crazy TV/film hours, about having children. Aaron wound up traveling the globe when he was sent to Japan, Korea, and Toronto for animation projects—without me. I left my day job to be a full-time journalist who taught popular classes at night, but I was lonely.

When I was asked to speak at the Brooklyn college where George taught, I wanted to remeet him. Was he still youthful and athletic? Luckily I was nothing like the chain-smoking mess George had last seen crying hysterically on the street corner, after he said he was sleeping with Diana, the wannabe actress.

I feared I'd become more bourgeois, heavier, made up, wearing the diamond ring and watch my husband had bought me. (Had I worn Aaron's gifts to remind me of his generosity, or that I was taken?) I asked a student where the journalism department was. She looked at me, pointed, and said, "That way, ma'am." I felt old and sweaty.

Aside from shorter hair, George looked startlingly the same. When we'd dated, I'd become thinner, tanner, more athletic, turning into him, wearing his uniform: faded jeans and crisp white shirts. Someone once stopped us on the street to say what a beautiful couple we made. Not a compelling reason to pledge your life to somebody. Yet for a cerebral girl usually locked in her mind, our year together still seemed dazzling.

"Time for coffee?" I asked him after my talk.

"You don't drink coffee," he remembered. "How about a campus tour?"

"Sure, why not?" I said casually. He didn't have to know that every morning for a year after he left, I opened my eyes, saw he wasn't there, and started crying. That was why it took me so long to sleep with Aaron; there had been a love overlap.

I learned that George's wife was Melissa, a Brooklyn teacher my age, not the Diana Slut of my old diaries. Aaron and I had beaten them to the altar. George took a picture from his wallet of his son. Aaron and I were childless; George's baby seemed to trump me. George asked about my parents, who didn't like him since his visit to the Midwest, where he'd slept in a tent on our lawn. He was continuing on to the Belize jungle and wanted to test the equipment he'd carried with him in his backpack.

I recalled that when Aaron first came to Michigan, he'd schlepped

Katz's Deli pickles, pastrami, and chopped liver on the plane as a present for my parents—who'd adored him from the start. My three brothers, who'd seen Aaron's TV shows, joked that they liked him more than they liked me. Since unlike me, Aaron would eat anything, they took him for Michigan food delicacies, from Detroit's Coney Island hot dogs to Lebanese baba ghanoush to Mongolian barbecue.

"Did you notice I quit smoking?" I asked George.

"I stopped five years ago," he said.

I had been smoke-free for only six months; he'd won that one, too.

I felt competitive and kept comparing my old boyfriend with me and my new husband. When I'd said "I do," I was following my brain, my friends, my family, my therapist. But I'd never fully recovered from the George heartbreak. I told myself I was the overly sensitive type who never got over anything. When I had last-minute doubts, I got down the aisle by realizing that if it didn't work out, I'd rather my obituary said "divorced" than "never been married."

I felt like I'd never see George again. Yet seven years after our split, there was unfinished business. "So what really happened between us?" I asked.

"Oh, Sue," he said. "I was so immature and stupid and incapable back then."

That felt better than his previous final words, after he'd found Diana, lost his Jane Street sublet, and called to say, "I want my bed frame back." Enraged that he'd cared more about twenty dollars' worth of wood than me, I'd said, "I'll burn it on your lawn."

Now I added, "In retrospect, we were too different," wishing I had a cigarette.

Before I left, George threw out nice images. The black bikini I wore in Negril. The poem I'd written where George was a bronzed fish, fluttering around the deep. He leaped off white cliffs, shouted, "Eels! Barracudas!" and brought back treasures: striped shells, brain coral. I was sunburned, hiding in the shade with a stack of books, reading too much, the way Aaron did.

"Aaron and I went to Jamaica on our honeymoon," I let slip.

"Yeah, I've been back a million times," George retaliated.

Right before we split up, I'd visited George at work. Hand in hand in the moonlight, he'd shown me a line of houses on the water and said, "Wouldn't it be amazing to live in a brownstone here someday?"

"I didn't leave Michigan to live in Brooklyn," I'd said, without thinking. Now I understood what my words meant. George was from Brooklyn; his wife was, too. So was Diana, whom he'd given a role in his play. If I'd wanted to be in Brooklyn drama, could I have wed George? Suddenly it seemed my choice to move on, not his. Maybe it was the feeling of being a young, athletic hippie-artist-rebel that I missed more than I missed him.

"It's nice to see you back in Brooklyn," George said.

I was glad to reconnect, with the benefit of time, wisdom, and a wedding ring. When the car service arrived I hugged him good-bye, then boarded my black chariot back to Manhattan.

"The campus is on the water," I told Aaron later that night, sliding next to him on the couch, wishing he liked to swim. "It's kind of pretty."

Aaron put his arm around me, kissed me on the lips. "Can't see you in Brooklyn," he said.

Last night, reading the newspapers with my feet on Aaron's lap as he gave me a blissful foot massage with his warm hands, I suggested a foreign vacation for our upcoming fifteenth anniversary.

"Work is too busy in July," he mumbled.

About to be upset, I remembered that Aaron had accompanied me on the Los Angeles leg of my book tour when I'd needed him, even though he hated L.A. We'd flown to Chicago when I was worried about my youngest brother, Michael, leaving his job. Aaron canceled work commitments last second to hop a plane to Michigan when my father had a heart attack, the same way he'd rushed to Westchester when his father was in the hospital. To take care of people he loved, he'd travel, fast, with no hesitation. Meanwhile I was the one who had taken my time to fall madly in love and lust with my mate.

Now I looked around our Manhattan apartment, filled with joy. Pictures of us lined the shelves next to Aaron's TV/film scripts and my books, which he'd help me go from reading to reviewing to writing. I felt so thankful that I'd wound up with the right husband, a man who flunked honeymoons but aced marriage.

The First Year

JILL KARGMAN

I spent my wedding night with Russell Crowe.

Harry had passed out after we (gag) "consummated" the marriage, which we did because, despite our extreme exhaustion at 1 a.m. after the candle-covered wedding of my dreams, that's whatcha do. Not that I didn't want to—I did; it's just that I was totally wiped out but felt there was some sort of medieval edict that said we had to bang and seal it all in somehow. Not that anyone would be waving my flag-of-Japan newly nonvirginized bedsheet in the town square or anything, but I figured, we gotta deal.

Naturally, per alleged male biology, newly minted hubby passed out while I was staring at the ceiling in a haze of surreal snapshots of the twinkling, romantic evening. I looked down at my hand. I still felt that with my manicure and chunk o' ice, I looked like someone chopped off the hand of some older lady and glued it onto my wrist stump.

So there I was, wide-awake with the remote control. Flip, flip . . .

home shopping, flip flip . . . *Full House,* flip flip . . . *Gladiator.*
BINGO. I lay back, and somehow this hundredth viewing was so
much more emotional. A welling sadness rose within my chest until I
burst into tears with full-on audible sobs. They fucking KILLED HIS
KID? And RAPED HIS WIFE AND FUCKING TOLD HIM
ABOUT IT?! I wanted to bash Joaquin's harelippy face in. And this
was before he got all psycho on *Letterman.* There was no way someone could be THAT talented an actor and master evil so perfectly
without actually being the apex of douchebaggery in real life. At least
that's what they all said about Brenda on *90210* back in the day.
Beeyotch on-screen, satanic in life. Finally, in the end, I felt my
esophagus closing as a golf-ball-size lump rose in my throat, and by
the time Russell bites it to allegedly join his dead fam in A Better
Place, I was a rocking snotball of a mess.

Not to be a total drama queen read into this shit, but maybe in
some small way I felt a new chapter coming upon me in that 3 a.m.
moment, a crossing over. No, I wasn't married off in some kind of
horrifying barter system for chattel, I was in love and ecstatic—but I
still found that despite my elation from the best night of my life at that
point, I felt a twinge of sadness that was coaxed out by the jeering
Roman Colosseum.

I'd seen it all a ton of times (I'm big on high-budget Hollywood
flicks. Extra credit for period shit), but somehow this time I was so
much more hysterical. Maybe because I was channeling the swirling
amorphous sea of my own feelings bubbling up inside me into a reaction to Russell's tragic journey. I was so so so elated to be married to
Harry. And yet there was a slight melancholy about flushing my maiden
name, Kopelman. We had agreed I'd gladly take his name, Kargman—
I wanted the same name as my future litter of little of nuggets. I didn't

know why now I was a lip quiverer; for crying out loud, it wasn't some whole new identity with unpronounceable fifty consonants jammed together or something. It was the same jewy-jewstein vibe and identical towel initials and paper monogram—*JK*. It was almost the exact name, just with the "opel" swapped out for "arg." Not a BFD. I was more than thrilled to see Alison, my seventies middle moniker, swirl down the bowl forever, but my last-name change somehow felt like I was leaving my parents and entering this new family.

I decided I couldn't lie there in bed. I got up and walked through the long marble hallway of my Jay-Z suite.

Wait, let me back up.

The day before my wedding, I'd arrived with all my stuff to find my very sweet tiny one-bedroom hotel setup. It had a little living room area so that my bridesmaids could get their makeup done while we all sipped some champers from room service before the big event. After the rehearsal dinner, a few of my gals and my gay BFF, Trip, came over to tuck me in. We had a drink and hugged, and they left at about 2 a.m. so we all could get down to beauty rest.

I turned out the lights, and as I started to melt into the zillion-thread-count sheets and yummy hotel pillow fest, I heard a loud scratching sound from the wall that was very clearly some furry life-form.

The blood froze in my veins. Great. I called downstairs and tried to calmly explain in the most anti-Bridezilla, pleasant voice I could conjure, that I was very sorry to bother them, but there was BECLAWED RODENTIA BURROWING near me and that I WAS GETTING MARRIED TOMORROW. They sent up a dude who put his ear to the wall, listened to the hairball mystery menace, casually walked to the phone, and dialed downstairs.

"Yeah, hi, we got a Code Eleven."

The next thing I knew, three butlers literally in tails (à la morning coat, not wall rat) carried all my belongings—including my wedding dress, which was stuffed like a dead body—to my new room: the Fifth Avenue Imperial Suite. The joint would make the late great Michael Jackson and his entourage of nannies, kids, handlers, and elephant bones gasp. It was insane. Ten rooms, a sprawling marble kitchen, a dining table for twelve, a princess bed, and a gilded rococo writing desk worthy of signing bills into laws with a feather plume.

So there I was, on my wedding night, wandering the grand apartment alone. I walked to the desk and opened the drawers, retrieving a piece of engraved watermarked hotel stationery. I sat down.

Dear Mom and Dad, I began.

Tears flowed with the ink as I thanked them for the most enchanting of weddings. It was all so ethereal and sublime, and during my toast of gratitude on the dance floor, I morphed into Halle Berry's Oscar speech, mascara cataracts and moved beyond measure, despite not being a blactress breaking boundaries. Just a bride. Who loved everyone in the room.

I wrote them that even though my name was changing, nothing else would. I would always be their BG (baby girl). I wept for twenty minutes straight until I signed *dotter* (tradition), and then something happened. I stopped crying. I folded the paper into thirds, stuck it in the envelope, and as I sealed it, I also closed the flap on my worries. I was Mrs. Harry Kargman now. And I was so glad.

Neither Russell nor the lump in my throat returned—the next few months brought blissful travels—our honeymoon in Italy and a business trip for Harry in Tokyo for ten days.

I'd decided to pursue a writing assignment, so I couldn't accompany him and scored a travel piece on then up-and-coming Cat Street for a travel magazine. We had a blast. I loved my new name on my passport. I loved being a unit. It was as if our first three months of marriage had shampoo-bottle-esque simple directions: Eat. Drink. Have Sex. Sleep Late. Repeat.

We came home and settled in. We enjoyed fun dinners with friends, and many weekends away for other people's weddings, which always seemed to reinforce our vows and make us reminisce about our own ceremony. We were feeling happily adjusted to married life. Harry was working round the clock, but I was busy as well and we were cocooned in a sweet bubble of self-indulgence and fun times, grinning with a newlywed glow.

And then one day I was sitting by the computer when I started to feel my boobs like . . . buzzing. I put my hands on my chest and m'knockers felt tender and firmer than usual. I must be PMSing.

And then it suddenly dawned on me . . . Oh boy . . . or girl.

I ran downstairs to Zitomer's "Department Store" (read: glorified pharmacy, but I love it anyway) and felt my heart pounding like timpani played by a cracked-out six-year-old. There they were: the pregnancy tests. I always remarked to friends when we saw them that people are either praying for a yes or praying for a no. But what was I? Neither, kinda. I bought First Response because they had the most commercials, so their media buyer won my arm reach to their product. I paid with a weird face on, like a smiley face whose smile has a squiggly line like it might barf. I went upstairs and pulled down the Calvins and peed on the stick. I was supposed to leave it in the stream for fifteen seconds or something. Gross. Okay, done. I decided to rest it on the cappy thing it came in and pace in the foyer. After two minutes, I busted back in and there it was clear as a nose job on a Horace Mann girl: Plus Sign. Holy-shit. Knocked up. Bun in the oven. Casting my own Mini-Me. Child Star waiting in the green womb. With child. (How archaic.)

Despite that positive + screaming at me like the Bat signal in the Gotham night sky, I went back down to Zitomer's and bought three more tests, all different brands. As my bladder is roughly the size of a lima bean, there's always pee at the ready. I dropped trou and covered the three tips. *Shwing! Shwing! Shwing!* All three poz. I thought I was going to explode. I didn't know what to do. So I put my coat back on and went back to Zitomer's.

To the kids' area. I looked at the shrunken stuff and footie pajamas and diapers and bottles and was reeling. Then my jaw dropped as I spied two tiny booties with lions on them. Eureka! Because of his fluffy mane of curly hair, I'd begun calling Harry "LC" for Lion Cub back when we had first starting dating. And here I was, with a tinier cub in my tummy. I bought the booties and had them gift-wrapped. And then I paced, waiting for him to come home.

When he texted me that he was out of the subway and headed back, I couldn't contain myself. I ran down the block and met him on the corner. He looked surprised to see me, especially with my hand holding a bow-covered box.

"Hi! What're you doing here? What's this?" he asked.

"Open it!"

It had originally crossed my mind that I could put all the various pregnancy tests in a box with ribbon to tell him that way, but then it occurred to me it was grody and creepsville to hand him my urine.

His eyes widened as he pulled them out.

"NO!"

"Yes!"

We hadn't been trying. But we were lazy asses, so it wasn't a total shock. I wasn't into Jimmy Jackets and neither was he. I called the condies—even his allegedly imperceptible lambskin ones—raincoats. So we bagged whenever I was riding the crimson wave. Or just finished it. Or didn't feel like schlepping to rifle through the drawer for a dick hat.

So there we were on the corner of Seventy-sixth and Park in the autumn night. Uh . . . oops.

I guess it's true, that joke . . ." I said.

"What joke?" he asked.

"Do you know what they call people who use the Withdrawal Method?"

"What?"

"Parents."

. . . .

So only a few months into our marriage, I would grow into a fatty. We were both twenty-eight, and while I was lying like a beached whale on the couch eating Ben & Jerry's, my friends were dancing on tables at Bungalow 8. While they were primping in size-four dresses for a night on the town, I was watching the circumference of my thighs expand by the day. Them: Barneys. Me: Buybuy Baby.

Harry and I immediately felt plunged from one club—married folk—into the new world of parents. There was a new lingo we didn't know, about Bumbos and Diaper Genies and all this crap we supposedly NEEDED. I looked at the airplane-hangar-size space and asked him what the fuck our parents did without all this crap? The way everyone talked about these special bottles and organic this and that, you'd think it was a miracle people survived anywhere else.

I started to panic when I went to a baby shower of a fancy-pants acquaintance and all these women were talking about nursery schools and parenting books. I wasn't going to read fucking parenting books! Snooze! What, was I supposed to cancel my *Vogue* subscription and sign up for *Family Circle* now? No fucking way! I got scared my identity might get funneled into the fetus.

Then one woman sent me off into a tizzy.

Beeyotch: "You're getting a C-section, right?"

Me: "Uh . . . not that I know of, no."

B: "You're kidding, right? Oh no, no, no, no, no. You must get an elective C. You get your blowout and your manicure, it's all very civilized, no grunting, no sweating, you walk in, and they slice 'n' dice, and you get your baby in two minutes! And if you ask, I'm sure your doctor will do it a few weeks early so you don't have to deal with those last weeks of weight gain."

Me: silent, jaw on floor.

B: "Trust me, Jill, do it. Your husband will thank you for it, ifyaknowhatimean."

I walked away shaking. She made it sound as if my vag would be the Holland Tunnel and that if I didn't get a C, I might as well be some mammal in the woods squatting down and shitting out a baby. Panicked, I went to my gyno, who told me I was insane and that she didn't perform Cesareans unless it's an emergency.

I got over the fears of the birth and tried to just be in the moment and enjoy the pregnancy. No such luck. I puked my brains out and felt so exhausted it was as if I had taken three Ambiens and then had to have my day. But in the end, as my first anniversary approached, I realized my pregnancy really helped us nest and was a fire under my (fat) ass to really make a home. Soon we would be a family, and I couldn't defer dealing with the Crate & Barrel explosion that was my bachelorette pad, so we signed a lease on a fourth-floor walk-up and painted the baby's room yellow since we decided not to know the sex (which seems so weird in retrospect and I hate when people do that). As the painters were coating the apartment with paint, we decided to get away for our anniversary. Harry surprised me with a weekend at the Wheatley in the Berkshires, the hotel where we got engaged. We holed up and I got a prenatal massage and we ate like pigs and slept like the dead. After our first night, we told the manager how much fun we'd had and that maybe we'd make it an annual family tradition.

"I'm afraid that won't be possible," he said looking at my swollen tummy. "There are no children under ten allowed."

Oh well.

The next night, my actual anniversary, I ate so much I felt like I was prego with twins—my actual nugget and the food baby. Harry fell asleep and I lay awake again, staring at the ceiling. What a difference a year makes. My wedding night felt both five minutes and five years ago. So much had gone down. And it was amazing to imagine what the next year would bring.

Ghosts of Husbands Past

JUDITH MARKS-WHITE

My husband, Mark, and I arrived at the marital altar like beasts of burden dragging behind us remnants of our past—the overweight baggage of two respective lives. No longer were we the wide-eyed newlyweds of our twenties on the precipice of new beginnings. Slightly frayed around the edges though cautiously optimistic, we approached our first year ready to secure the old knots that had become unraveled and try another marriage on for size.

There is a certain comfort in going the matrimonial route after one has muddled through one's midlife crisis. By now, we had two things going for us: (1) life experience, and (2) well-oiled resiliency. Wounds from previous relationships had healed, or so I thought. The battle scars—our medals—were displayed proudly as proof that we had survived a handful of adversities, and were willing to go another round.

Mark, I soon learned, made smooth transitions, segueing from one marriage to the next like a bird in flight, flitting from nest to nest, and approaching each wife like a shiny new car waiting to be road-tested and broken in. I was his latest model. His colorful and illustrious nuptial past became a family joke. At our wedding in 2002, his brother David's toast resonates still as he echoed the all-familiar and rather startling refrain: "Mark just keeps getting married . . . and married . . . and married."

I was not amused.

Our histories, equally diverse and tinged with loss, were circumstantially different. Mark had three previous wives to my two husbands. The first, the father of my only child, was all but a distant memory. Ken and I parted ways after five years when our daughter, Elizabeth, was three. He later remarried a flight attendant with whom he developed a "meaningful relationship" thirty thousand feet above the Pacific. I imagined she had won his heart on frequent bicoastal trips by serving him an excess of minibar selections and unlimited bags of salted peanuts and by her ability to sashay down the 747 American Airlines aisle with such panache that he couldn't resist. The strawberry-blond hair didn't hurt either. Where she undulated with sensual dexterity—in high heels, no less—I would have suffered altitude sickness. Her wifely profile was so vastly removed from mine we might have inhabited different planets.

After a while Ken's image became a blurry snapshot slightly out of focus and bearing no resemblance to anyone I had ever intimately known. He simply faded into oblivion, surfacing only for parental purposes when joint decisions demanded our mutual attention. Years later, with our daughter grown and herself a parent, her father and I met only on those rare occasions that forced us to share similar space. The first time was Liz's wedding, when both of us, in a boozy haze, reunited like two long-lost relatives who couldn't quite place each other's face.

This "starter husband" never would have been had I been the woman I eventually came to be. No longer would I be attracted to Ken or him to me, but back in 1963, a year out of college and beginning a career in journalism, I turned to marriage as another rung in the ladder of prescribed protocol—a stepping-stone that officially marked the end of childhood and the start of what I perceived adulthood to be.

It was also a time when the first tremors of women's lib were struggling to break through, but weren't fully realized. Betty Friedan was not yet a household word, though her book *The Feminine Mystique* was starting to cause ripples, becoming the latest discussion at dinner parties. Home and hearth were still the expected MO of "nice girls" who were supposed to be virgins when they married.

There we were, Ken and I, registering at Georg Jensen, Bloomies', and Tiffany, playing out our assigned roles as Mr. and Mrs. Newly Married Couple, teetering on the edge of our own naïveté like two ill-prepared soufflés about to fall at any moment.

After our lavish wedding reception, dressed in my going-away suit and pillbox hat, we sat in the Oak Bar of the Plaza Hotel sipping glasses of Veuve Clicquot and feeling very grown up while we counted our envelopes of money surreptitiously handed to us by those guests who bypassed the registry items by showering us with cash.

The next morning we left for Puerto Rico, where, on the third day of our honeymoon, in the lobby of the Caribe Hilton Hotel, I ran into an old boyfriend who looked remarkably fit and more handsome than I had remembered, making me wonder if I had, perhaps, hopped on the marriage bandwagon too quickly. In comparison with Bob's muscular biceps bulging through his Izod shirt, my groom looked bleached and thin.

Instead, I dismissed that thought and settled into honeymoon mode, drank piña coladas on the white, sandy beach of San Juan, and worked on my tan. Two years later our daughter was born. Three years after that, Ken and I—the happy little homemakers—divorced. I never looked back.

I have since come to view my marriages as analogous to a three-act play. The curtain falling on act one—which felt more like a dress rehearsal—was followed by a lengthy intermission. It rose again when, with a couple of ill-fated relationships behind me, I was to meet the love of my life.

Call it divine intervention, on which many of life's pivotal moments are based. On a frigid December morning in 1978, I stopped off at Oscar's Deli in Westport, Connecticut, where my daughter and I had moved from Manhattan. After several years of exploring the "meat-market" smorgasbord of possibilities, and having given up any notion of ever meeting Mr. Right, I literally tripped over him standing in line ordering a sesame bagel with a slathering of cream cheese.

Excusing myself for being so clumsy, I serendipitously found a seat on the banquette next to him, and squeezing in, my huge down parka squished between us, I pulled out my prop: the latest novel I was reading. I began flipping pages, pretending to be engrossed but completely aware of his presence. A few minutes later, turning to me, he uttered the words that were ultimately to be repeated for years to come when people asked how we met.

"I don't know if it matters," he said, "but that book you're reading is upside down."

I was hooked.

It was a year after that chance encounter that Mort and I were married. Elizabeth's status as only child evolved into stepsister to Mort's three college-age children, who welcomed this fourteen-year-old into the fold with open arms, and just the right amount of sibling rivalry to keep it interesting. Liz played out her "new kid on the block" role with teenage delight, while they enjoyed having a new partner in crime to corrupt. And, a new family was born.

What had become my most significant relationship to date ended abruptly in January 1995, when we had just returned from visiting friends on Cape Cod, Mort threw back his head on our living room couch and died. The suddenness was stupefying as I was catapulted from wife to widow in the drawing of his final breath. Grief-stricken, I went through the next hours in a numbed state of disbelief. Surrounded by family and friends, who helped guide me through the unfathomable mystery of death, I could hardly process the depth of its grip that held me captive by its enormity.

There had been no warning signs, no sudden jolt of recognition that something big was about to happen. Much in the same way Mort had appeared in my life seventeen years earlier, he dramatically left without so much as a good-bye. His heart had simply given out.

After that, and for a long time following, the color drained from my life. I entered a monochromatic world fueled only by memory while the present felt oddly surreal—the future nonexistent. It was my work, my writing and teaching, that exonerated me from alienation into a routine that allowed me to move through my days in a somnambulant stupor—my survival mechanism between what no longer was and the vague uncertainty of tomorrow.

Dinner invitations from friends guaranteed I wouldn't be alone, but did not promise a reprieve from loneliness. For that there was no remedy. I had entered a new phase of my life, assuming the role of widow-in-training. Graciously, and with some trepidation, I gave myself over to those quick to respond by making me their new project.

I visited a chalet in Vermont, where skiing was to become my antidote for depression. I wasn't a skier. A mountain house in the Blue Hills of Virginia presented a similar escape from solitude. By spring, the first honeysuckle appeared. I was whisked off to a lakeside cottage in New Hampshire by friends whose sole purpose was to get me out of my doldrums and cook elaborate meals that would cushion the blow of my recent loss. Instead, I gained three pounds and felt sad. I took long walks on windy beaches and came down with a bad cold. Pretending to be grateful for their concern, I slipped into a kind of anesthetic inertia indicative of the grieving process. I brought along my laptop to record my feelings should an impromptu cathartic moment present itself. I wrote my weekly humor column, met freelance-article deadlines, and worked on my first novel that hadn't yet seen the light of day.

I became a regular traveler, zigzagging between my real life and the escape routes provided by others. My suitcase, a constant companion, eased me into role of rotating houseguest. I spent time with my gallery of friends, who introduced me to the rhythm of their lives, and the myriad activities that went along with them—all perfect distractions for keeping sadness at bay as I became a temporary resident in other people's lives.

Then, like an unwelcome intruder, late-August breezes appeared. Sweaters replaced halter tops, and the first subtle whisper of autumn crept in. It was time to put away porch furniture and throw an extra blanket on the bed. And suddenly it was over. I officially bade farewell to those halcyon days that had been a temporary buffer against my melancholy. I packed my bags, returned home, and silently mourned.

Time, the great equalizer, has a way of, if not completely obliterating gloom, at least of tempering it. If the life force is strong enough, emotional rehabilitation is possible, and slips in subtly like a sliver of sunlight breaking through a cloudy landscape. Eventually, the sting of bereavement ceased to be a sharp knifelike thrust and modulated into a dull ache and then to sporadic twinges that become bearable. Slowly, I emerged from my blackout, the color returning to my life.

The next months, Mort's memory continued to buoy me, so that his nonpresence became pervasive, as though a friendly ghost had taken up residence in the house. I had only to glance at the photos of us lining the shelves, and we were, once again, reunited. It was enough to hold me for a while. I fell in line like a good soldier standing guard over my own life. Weary from battle fatigue, I forged ahead as if nothing were particularly wrong, though not quite right either.

"What choice do you have," a friend asked, "but to keep going?"

But there were choices, plenty of them. I could fall apart, cave in under the heaviness of my grief. I could surrender to the comfort of apathy or enter a new relationship.

Change occurs when you aren't looking. Act three's curtain rose in 2000 when, just back from a few days away, I was invited to a last-minute dinner party hosted by friends who lived in Manhattan and summered in Westport. The purpose, aside from Mimi's desire for any opportunity to cook, was to introduce a group of her available female friends to a recently separated and on the-fringe-of-divorce bachelor: a Florida import up for the weekend. On a warm July evening, we assembled at Mimi and Michael's house for Mark to assess the harem of hotties and choose from this bevy of postmenopausal divas the one who would make the cut as his weekend companion. Underwhelmed, I agreed to attend.

Shrouded in a shield of ambivalence, I managed to sport a to-die-for outfit and coquettish air that interested Mark enough to call me the next day to invite me to dinner. I had plans. Monday, back in Florida, he asked if he could fly up to see me the following weekend. I casually agreed, feeling mildly amused and flattered, as though I had taken first place in a competitive event whose prize—a man—seemed, at the time, more of a liability than a treasured acquisition.

That Saturday night, Mark and I sat over dinner at a Thai restaurant exploring the menu along with each other's life. He had four daughters. I had one. His grandchildren numbered double digits. I had two. He was a Virgo. I was an Aries—a killer combo. We both loved films, although my passion bordered on addiction. I was a theater buff; Mark, a jazz enthusiast. He could play the piano by ear, but couldn't read music. I could whip up a poem for a birthday party in a couple of hours. We both liked strawberry milk shakes. Neither of us had a burning desire to hike. We could recite passages from favorite childhood poems and Gilbert and Sullivan operettas. It was an evening of discovery fraught with the warm realization somewhere between the appetizer and dessert that we were, quite possibly, made for each other.

Along with that scenario were fifteen hundred miles between us that rendered us geographically undesirable, providing the perfect safety net: long-distance dating without infringing on each other's autonomy.

And so, gradually, we settled into a routine as frequent fliers on JetBlue. Where many years earlier my first husband had stumbled upon love in the friendly skies, I was now doing regular runs to the

Fort Lauderdale airport. One week I flew south, the next Mark came to Westport. We were introduced to each other's gallery of friends, and before long we became "an item."

Six months later, having crossed over that fine line between dating and what was referred in high school as "going steady," I announced with stoic determination: "I'm never moving to Florida."

He was not a cold-weather person, but was open to new adventures, I being his latest one.

Until now, we had been careful not to use the M-word, though the whiff of it hung heavy in the air. A year later, an engagement ring adorned my finger. Mark relocated to Connecticut, moved into my house, and we married in June at Stonehenge—a lovely inn in Ridgefield, Connecticut—set among wildflowers and a babbling brook, where, surrounded by family and friends all wishing us well, we embarked on this new chapter in our lives.

When a door slams shut on a divorce, it's different from the one that closes quietly after a death. Divorce's ending is noisy and jarring—an intrusion into life's rhythm with painful repercussions that can last indefinitely, dissipating when both parties move on to new relationships.

The aftermath of Mort's death was daunting—relinquishing its hold unimaginable. I had burrowed into a place where apathy seemed not only familiar but oddly comforting. Mort's presence had become an invisible fixture: photos, his art, a medicine chest filled with his prescriptions, drawers spilling over with miscellaneous paraphernalia, after-shave cologne whose scent still lingered, and closets that still housed his suits and ties I hadn't been willing to discard—relics of a life still in progress that ended all too soon.

Added to these were Mark's possessions—items divided between him and his former wife. Our home became a warehouse that bulged with accessories and merged furniture, Mark's baby grand piano and bass, his art collection that demanded wall space on which hung Mort's illustrations and portraits. What was his and mine now became ours as we tiptoed around each other like two intimate strangers taking up space in the same house.

And then there was the matter of the cat—my beloved Annabelle—adopted sixteen years earlier by Mort and me from a litter of felines at the Humane Society. Mark, I soon discovered, was allergic to cat dander, necessitating Annabelle's move to a new home and compounding my already existing feelings of loss.

There was a tug of despair when one day Mark announced in a moment of impulsive rancor that too much of Mort was lingering in corners. It seemed wrong, unnatural. It was time to discard the tangible evidence that another person once dwelled in spaces into which my new husband was trying to fit. Like a well-mannered hostess wanting to please her permanent houseguest, I rearranged furniture, put in a new kitchen, and relegated boxes of memorabilia to the basement to be buried among the old discarded mementos, erasing all traces of my former marriage.

I viewed Mark as a "substitute husband," replacing the real one, whose absence seemed a glaring omission. And so began our first year, where we juggled between past and present, trying to blend into each other's life like pieces of a jigsaw puzzle that didn't quite fit together.

In order for any marriage to spread it swings and fly, it needs a blank canvas on which to paint a new picture. Not, as Lillian Hellman described in *Pentimento,* one where old transparencies of former images peek through the cracked paint.

We entered our version of "couple's boot camp"—a period of

adjustment—where we settled into domesticity, and transitioned from whirlwind dating into a less frenetic routine. I secretly missed my bimonthly flights to Florida, a place I had come to view as a mini–vacation retreat. Accustomed as I was to dining out or ordering take-out, suddenly Mark expected me to cook. I preferred grabbing a bite when the mood struck. Where I had dabbled at golf on my Florida visits, I had no intention of doing eighteen holes in Connecticut. Mark's interest in bridge soon became an obsession, starting with Monday and Thursday nights and moving on to Wednesday after-noons. I pored over *Bridge for Dummies*—a study in futility. For me, card games were what I imagined people did to fill up their time, serving no real purpose other than to satisfy a hedonistic urge.

Mark, an engineer and software developer, had become a com-puter nerd, spending hours locked away doing spreadsheets and mak-ing deals with printing companies interested in his estimating program. He required little sleep, often rising before dawn and on the phone with customers by eight o'clock. I could hear him in the next room—his makeshift office—and unaccustomed to having a man lurking underfoot, I grew to resent the lack of privacy that now invaded my once-quiet sanctuary.

Conversely, Mort, a commercial illustrator, had a studio in town where he went each morning, returning at night, with a break when we met for lunch. Now my writing routine was stifled, and the silence on which I had come to rely was being sporadically interrupted. I left the house to find solace at a favorite restaurant where I retreated daily to write or meet friends for lunch, and where I, eventually, completed and later sold two novels.

The idiosyncratic habits of everyday life—traits we once found endearing—morphed into annoying: Mark devoured Oreos in bed, leaving crumbs embedded in the sheets. I ate oranges, discarding the rinds with wild abandon. I left threads of dental floss on the night table. He clipped his toenails on the toilet and cut his own hair, leaving strands of it in the bathroom sink. He had a postnasal drip and snored. I took to rolling my eyes. I stole the blankets. He wouldn't share pillows. He talked during movies. I secretly detested the argyle socks that he wore for all occasions. His saddle shoes (his trademark) seemed pretentious. I slept with a stuffed animal. He preferred the windows closed in summer with the air conditioner blasting. His ex-wife designed quilts. I couldn't sew on a button. He loved cruises. I got seasick. He told bad jokes, and worse, he awakened each morning with a cheery demeanor, while I didn't come alive until after breakfast . . . The list, along with our resentments, grew longer with every passing month until our first year seemed more of a struggle than a loving partnership built on commonality.

My friends were cordially obliging, graciously welcoming Mark as the new man in my life with some minor alterations. No longer could I purge my grief over dinners; nor did they console. Trips down Memory Lane that we once had rehashed with great pleasure—couples vacations, moments shared, inside jokes—were no longer possible in Mark's presence. We were guarded now, choosing topics that were politically correct and couple-friendly.

During our courtship, Mark and I had found our diverse interests to be opportunities to widen our scope. Now these became deterrents, serving only to accentuate the gap between us. It was no longer cute to think that "opposites attract." I craved the duality I had with Mort: easy, relaxed, accepting. Mark's view of being a couple and mine were vastly different. He was a type A personality, who seemed more controlling than compliant; I, a free spirit, who took oversensitivity to the level of an art form. He was linear and cautious; I, more spontaneous and open. I saw us as two mismatched bookends holding up a rickety marriage, whose expectations might never be met.

And suddenly the honeymoon was over.

Ideally, I had hoped our first year would be steeped in wedded bliss—the blending of two souls blessed to have found each other. Instead, I was haunted by old ghosts—the emotional tentacles of my past. I was married to Mark, and had brought Mort along for the ride. Old memories latched on, infiltrating my life with unrelenting force, keeping me a prisoner as I gnawed on the carcass of my previous marriage, refusing to breathe new life into my new one and validate its existence.

Time has a way of either diluting or exaggerating the truth. The reality was that Mort hadn't been perfect; neither was I, nor was our marriage. Our first year was a time of extensive marital housecleaning and adjustments. Although we did evolve into something that was as close to compatible as I had ever known, it was through the trail of years that we had blossomed and endured. We also had one basic ingredient that Mark and I had yet to experience: a shared history— a marriage's greatest gift.

If life is kind, it often gives us second chances; third chances rarely. One day, toward the end of our first year, we became weary of it all— worn down—and for the first time the baggage we had been lugging around seemed excessively cumbersome. The repetitive dance that we had so skillfully choreographed came to a screeching halt. Both of us needed to take stock before we could move ahead. I was tired of being angry: angry at Mort for dying; at Mark for not being Mort; mostly angry at myself for idealizing Mort to my advantage by punishing my new husband for not measuring up to a phantom husband.

It was time to stop living in a past masquerading as my future.

If, in fact, "past is prologue," then we are the sum total of all our experiences, and the players who have impacted our lives carry us along on this incredible journey. The two men I had married brought me to where I was now, giving me that third chance to reinvent my life and get on with the business of marriage.

What Mark and I needed most was a springboard from which to take off, unencumbered by past demons, and create a history of our own. But before that was possible, I needed to say good-bye to Mort—an opportunity I never had—even more, to put closure on us as a couple. Similarly, it was time for Mark to accept what once was, namely Mort's and my marriage, not as a competition, but as a testimonial blueprint to all marriages past and future.

The week before our first-year anniversary nine years ago, Mark and I drove to Compo Beach. Summer had just arrived after a rainy spring. It was early evening and the sun was still high in the sky. Placing a blanket on the sand, we sat watching the waves break against the shore. Sailboats punctuated the horizon; children skipped along the water's edge ahead of their parents, delighting in the first taste of warm weather.

For me, summer was always a season of renewal when the days slowed, each one blending into the other like a giant, lazy yawn. Mark and I sat close until dusk settled in, enveloping us in a slate-blue backdrop, merging sky, sand, and water as though there were no dividing line between them, making it hard to tell where one left off and the other began.

Soon the early evening breezes kicked up and the beach emptied. It was just the two of us now, save for the seagulls that swooped down alongside our picnic basket, hoping to get lucky. Deciding to take a walk before supper, we sauntered along the water's edge—husband and wife in one shadow. I reached over and took Mark's hand as his closed over mine. The days were longer now. Our first year of marriage was nearly behind us, the old ghosts gently laid to rest. We had made it through.

As I pulled my sweater tightly against me, Mark wrapped his arm around my shoulder. It was a time of beginnings—of history in the making—as we continued down the long expanse of beach toward our hard-earned future so dearly won.

"There's Always Divorce" and Other Parental Advice

SALLY KOSLOW

My sons have put a ring on it. They are getting married. For months, the conversational axis in our households has tilted on diamond versus sapphire, tuxedo versus dark suit, and Costa Rica versus Jackson Hole, since the venue of Venus is booked. Not that my boys hold my opinions in especially high regard. As the mother of grooms, my primary function has been to stifle myself, ruminate on the true meaning of mother-in-law-hood, and write checks. After the Jurassic Bar Mitzvah era, my husband and I thought our major fiduciary responsibility for bash throwing was over, but—who knew?—today the groom's family goes halfsies on many expenses, and there are many.

From what I can tell, Jed and Rory have chosen their life partners well. I have grown attached to these almost-daughters, and after playing house, I'm glad they're going legal. Living together is fine—I did it myself—but one nasty fight and a call to Moishe's Movers later, both Anne and Kim could be out of my life.

For wedding number one, I bought a strapless column of Dolce & Gabbana satin so sleek and corseted I don't plan to eat as much as a scoop of ice cream between now and July. For wedding number two, which is next December, I hope to wear a dreamy velvet frock I pounced on at my one and only Chanel sample sale, justifying the purchase with that eternal salvo, "I'll wear it someday." Someday is around the corner, a son taking a wife. This brings me back—to that time before both boys sprouted wit and whiskers, before they arrived at all, to those starter years when my husband and I were twenty-three, younger than my kids are now, just married, and calling a bagel dinner so we could nap, then leave at eleven for Studio 54.

At twenty-three, some people are old oaks. They've fought wars, supported families, become parents, faced disasters, or at the very least skipped high school because they were too smart for their own good. At that age, Rob and I were not quite smart enough to get out of our own way. Our vision of married life was fuzzy. We were an unlikely couple: East Coast boy/Midwest girl, Hellmann's mayo/Miracle Whip, outgoing/shy, athletic/not. We bickered. We competed. We were young.

Rob and I were standard-issue, early-1970s types, though cut of different cloth. He was charming yet caustic, a suburban hippie with eyes the color of grass, the kind you mow, not the sort we smoked at college, where we'd dated for two years. Rob majored in French, a romantic yet useless choice unless you hoped to teach the language or work where it is spoken. He planned to do neither. He hadn't planned at all. After graduation, Rob returned to his parents' home near New York City and drove a cab. Every Sunday he made deliveries for a bakery, so the pint-size freezer in the kitchenette through which you squeezed into my similar-size apartment was always stuffed with jaw-breaking rugelach he received as a tip.

I was conventional yet career-oriented, a girl who'd moved from Fargo to Manhattan with a degree in English and her earnestness so intact that when Rob once suggested lunch at McDonald's because it was my "kind of place," I wept at the insult. He liked golf tournaments. I, *Masterpiece Theatre.* I couldn't understand what was funny about Woody Allen and he felt the same way about the news from Lake Wobegone.

Soon after I arrived in New York, an Alberta Clipper blew in from my mother, trumpeting the message "get the guy to marry you or move on." I'm not a lot of things, but I am determined, and took this direction to heart. Moving on, I decided, was unthinkable. Rob was more than my love. He'd become my roommate, my only close friend within fifteen hundred miles, and my Seeing Eye dog in a city of blinding confusion. I'd landed an editing job—back at college in Madison, Wisconsin, when not ducking the national guard as they teargassed Vietnam War protesters, I, with shame for my bourgeois ambition, had mailed résumés—but the fancy-pants atmosphere of the magazine where I worked scared the confidence right off me. Every night, Rob restored it, and even though both of us were embryonic, something told me he was the one. I'm not sure, however, why he stuck with me; we weren't caught in a maelstrom of nuptials. I suspect Rob believed that one day I would simply disappear, not turn to him every morning and ask, as I did, "Is this the day we're getting engaged?"

Had a woman ever tried this on one of my sons, she would have found me stalking her, assault weapon in hand. Forget The Rules. My approach was the kind of niggling, tone-deaf assault that ultimately can wear a man down. One August evening, as Rob and I drove to his parents' home, we pulled to the side of the road and he popped open a small velvet box that contained a sparkling rock. I don't recall if he actually asked me to marry him, but the next stop involved toasting with champagne at his parents' home. I later learned that the family had anticipated an epic engagement during which, I imagine, they hoped their son might, say, graduate from law school. But all of these people—and I add my name to the list—had underestimated my mother, a woman who knew how to seal a deal.

Nowadays a bride and groom become their own ecosystem. But decades ago, it was the mother of the bride's Woodstock. The bride chose her dress, a color scheme, and with her fiancé's input—assuming he was interested, which Rob was not—china and silver patterns. The groom showed up with a ring, hangover optional. My mother selected our wedding date and virtually everything else. Not once did Rob and I meet with a florist, a stationer, a caterer, a bandleader. This gave us ample time to wonder, *What have we gotten into?* Three months after the wedding train had left the station, I bared my cold feet to my father. Never one to confront my mother, his response was, "There's always divorce."

Rob and I were married on December 26 in North Dakota. The temperature never broke zero. Rob's family tells tales about how tears formed icicles on their eyelashes, how the hearty locals plugged cars into warming contraptions before they drove, and how while the New York guests bundled in full-length mink, bikini-clad Canadian tourists cavorted around the Holiday Inn pool as if they were catching rays in Barbados.

On Christmas, we got a special gift from the rabbi, whose wife had just dumped him. At a command-performance counseling session, he ranted about how most marriages crash over sex or money. Or both!

At the rehearsal an hour later, my future mother-in-law became incensed when the same rabbi forbid the exclamation point that had ended every other Jewish wedding for 5,732 years: the groom breaking a glass. I never fully understood the rabbi's beef, because I stopped listening after "hymen" and the shade that word turned my father's face. Rob developed a fever that spiked during the wedding ceremony. At the reception, a drunken couple danced to our song before we did. We did have a high old time on the trip back east, however, when a blizzard grounded our plane and a Minneapolis hotel put us up in their honeymoon suite. The detour didn't delay our real honeymoon because we hadn't planned one. We simply returned to our messy little dive and matching life.

None of this was an auspicious start to marriage, and it didn't get better when a few weeks later we were robbed in our brownstone's vestibule. My new husband handed over his wallet. I had just cashed my dainty fashion-magazine paycheck and peeled off two tens. "Give the guy all your fucking money!" Robert yelled. "He's pointing a knife at my back." Reluctantly, I complied.

After this, without discussing it, I decided that we needed a doorman. Back in the day, apartments were easy to come by in our neighborhood, where sensible people wouldn't park their cars, much less themselves. After looking for an hour with a broker, I announced to Rob that we were moving. The same day we signed a lease for a one-bedroom in a grand dowager building. Our apartment, which you entered through a genuine foyer, had a vast living room and cozy dining room, enormous closets, high ceilings, herringbone parquetry, bookshelves, arches, a bike room with a vending machine that sold milk, a laundry in the basement instead of blocks away, and a leafy view of Riverside Park. Recently, this apartment was listed for sale at $1.3 million, but when we were newlyweds, it cost $285 a month to rent.

We were excited about our new home, but when we changed addresses, we not only brought along our bad habits; we also seemed to adopt the other person's most odious traits. Rob learned to be relentless and I to be sarcastic. I also threw things. One evening, in response to a flying phone book, he tossed all my clothes in the hall and locked me out in my underwear. Good times.

And then he got mugged. Rob had segued from taxi hack to construction worker to real estate manager in the dodgiest part of the Bronx, where he was cornered in a boiler room, beaten by a junkie with a pipe, shot, and left for dead. His boss called my office and told me to go home and wait for further information. Why I didn't rush straight to the ER I can explain only by saying I was so stunned I felt as if I, too, had been conked on the head. I was also twenty-three going on thirteen, still doing whatever real adults instructed. A few hours later, to my immense relief, a bandage-swaddled Rob staggered into our apartment, his thrift-shop army jacket splattered with blood. The next night we threw a party for all our friends, where Rob held court and repeated his war story on a continuous loop

Perhaps the beating was divine intervention, mugging some sense into us. We rarely discussed it, but the incident was an elephant of a testimonial that whispered "grow up." Incrementally, we did. The process began by making a home. We stapled pink plaid sheets to our bedroom walls, had draperies sewn by an elf in a yarmulke on the Lower East Side, and ordered pinkalicious shag carpeting. The room looked very Pepto-Bismol meets Cinderella. Unaware that a product existed that stripped finish in minutes, Rob and I spent night after sweaty night sanding our cupboard doors, which we repainted egg-yolk yellow. We hung calico curtains—our kit had a win—unpacked wedding presents, and began to host dinner parties on our twelve place settings of Wedgwood Florentine and Gorham Buttercup sterling flatware. Our signature dish was Craig Claiborne's stuffed flank steak, though one night we threw an earsplitting disco party and served fried chicken in straw baskets lined with red bandanas. We were a colorful couple, doing what happy couples did. When our first anniversary rolled around, we celebrated at La Bibliothèque, a restaurant tricked out like a library. Seeing Rob through the candlelight, I realized I no longer felt spooked or tempted by my dad's term of endearment, "There's always divorce." We'd made it through the first year. Life could only get better, and it did.

Over the years, we have befriended many couples. Half of them have divorced, many of our friends are on round two or three of marriage, and several of my best buddies are single. Meanwhile, Rob and I are chugging along, the little engine that never surrendered. My husband doesn't look much different to me than he did in college, but inexplicably, soon we will celebrate our fortieth anniversary, on which I believe you're expected to exchange gift certificates to orthopedists and cosmetic surgeons. We are happy, very happy. In no way, however, do we define the charmed life.

During the decades, we've faced down the standard grab bag of health problems, deaths of parents, work setbacks, and—damn you, Rabbi—intermittent financial frustration. If you ask Rob, he'll say I still don't know how much milk to pour in his cereal, and yes, once I voted for Rudolph Giuliani. We aren't one of those couples who have hammered out a mission statement that ensures that we present ourselves like matched draft animals. We're nobody's role model, but I'm skeptical of public role models. Whenever I see couples behaving on cultlike autopilot, always in character—"You tell the story, Pooh bear!" "No, baby, you!"—what I think they reveal is their measure of devotion to self-control and branding, not necessarily each other. We are a different kind of team, still making it up as we go along, pissing each other off and sometimes acting bossy, critical, and small. But lubricating every childish act is laughter, which, at least 65 percent of the time, is not at the other's expense.

After this lifetime together, we share a common history, which is not small at all. Our story is filled with anecdotes, digressions, and footnotes that are goofy, tender, terrifying, and ours. How when we roasted our first turkey we chose a recipe that called for a crab-apple jelly glaze and had to use a hammer to crack the bird's shellac. (Never again have we served poultry as moist or as purple.) How numerous cigar-puffing uncles and fifty other near and dear ones crowded into our apartment and made seven pounds of Zabar's finest Nova Scotia salmon disappear in five minutes at the bacchanalia that was our oldest son Jed's bris. How after we drove my mother to the airport the next day we sang "Happy Days Are Here Again." They were. We had become a family. (Correction: a family and a nurse. In today's dollars, she would probably also cost $1.3 million.)

Some of our chapters are dull; others painful. We are awash in memories we can lip-synch, including some Rob and I could and would never explain to anyone. But this archive welds us, friends and lovers who've grown up together. Whenever I look at Rob, I see the boy in the man. Dammit, I love the guy.

That Jed and Rory are getting married is, for their generation, almost quaint; statistics point to cohabitation, not marriage. Recently, when one of their new friends discovered that both Rob and I were the parents, still married to each other, the shock on this kid's face made me feel as if we had just stumbled out of a diorama at the Museum of National History. Has our endurance made our boys more willing than many of their friends to go over the cliff to marriage? All I know is that we haven't scared them off.

Jed and Rory strike me as infinitely more prepared for matrimony than Rob and I were, though in fairness, they're far older: thirty-four and twenty-eight. They treat their fiancées with enormous consideration and respect, as they are treated in return. Teasing is gentle and infrequent. They make plans, many plans. Perhaps we should take lessons from them, not offer advice. But to a mother, advice giving is part of the job description, and so:

> *Think beyond the wedding to the life you want to build together. No one will remember if the groom wore a dark suit or a tuxedo.*

> *Don't measure yourself against the next couple. Be skeptical of others' perfection.*

> *Do everything you can to make sure your wives love your parents.*

> *Keep laughing.*

> *Put those dirty boxers in the hamper.*

> *Ladies, learn to roast a chicken.*

> *Never think, "There's always divorce."*

> *Call your parents. We finally know a thing or two.*

Juan and Martita

ABBY SHER

I'll admit, I was a little tipsy at our wedding. My cousin had nursed me on champagne before I walked down the aisle. It was the only way to soften that sharp pucker on my face as I heard the words *forever* or *death do us part*. It's not that I doubted my love for Jay. I just didn't know if I was ready to die next to him. My father had died in 1985 when I was eleven; my mother just a year before my wedding. Many of the same faces from her funeral surrounded us now, watching expectantly, eager to cheer and dance. But the only eyes I could focus on were Juan and Martita's.

Juan had a helmet of shiny black hair and boxy shoulders. His gaze was solemn yet bright. His cheek pressed firmly against Martita's. Martita—yellow blond with a block of solid tooth peeking out of her giddy smile. Her eyes were mischievously clear, the color of the Caribbean.

Juan and Martita were our cake toppers. Crafted from papier-mâché, I think. Maybe Play-Doh. I'll never know for sure. Jay and I got to keep them for just a few short months. They'd been traveling from wedding cake to wedding cake, passed on through a chain of friends and relatives—a Spanish tradition Jay's sister had adopted. As we took our first bite of vanilla frosting, I clutched the figurines in a greedy fist and swallowed sullenly. I knew it was our turn to pass them on to the next betrothed couple, and I couldn't bear letting them go.

I'd never been that attached to my dollies as a child. I had a favorite teddy bear with mismatched eyes and a music box in his rear end. But once his throat split and his yellow stuffing started leaking out, I retired him to a bookshelf. I never really clicked with Barbie and I tossed my plastic Smurf collection in a Dumpster when we cleaned out our childhood home. But Juan and Martita were more than toys. In the brief time I'd known them, I'd come to see them as my surrogate parents, my guardian angels.

They stood smiling on our mantel as Jay and I addressed invitations and planned seating arrangements. They were resolutely sunny, teeth ablaze with fierce optimism. A constant affirmation: you two can be as bright and inseparable as we are. Even though they weighed no more than a paperback book, I began to count on them, as if cemented to that perch. I came through the front door of our one-bedroom Brooklyn apartment and said hello to them before looking to see whether Jay was home, too.

I know my sister paid a lot for our wedding cake. With both of our parents deceased, she and my older brother struggled to make me feel like we were still a family. But I honestly have no recollection of what the cake looked or tasted like. All I knew was that once I gulped down that mixture of butter, flour, sugar, eggs, I would have to part with my newest security blanket. Jay took the microphone and called up our friends Sarah and Nate. I didn't know what to say to them as I extended my arm, knuckles tight around Juan's pink neck. I didn't have the voice for anything pithy anyway. All I could think of was how much I missed those tiny painted smiles already. I knew they were dolls made of paper and glue but their spines and souls felt stronger than mine.

Sarah was actually one of the few people I could connect to without censoring myself that first year of marriage. Sarah, Jay, and I had all worked together in Chicago and she'd watched us dating, then moving in together, and finally climbing into a U-Haul and heading to New York. I kept Sarah for her rendition of what had happened.

We were really happy together, right?

He's so in love with you, Ab.

Maybe because she was thousands of miles away now, we confided in each other via long e-mails, unloading words that were too heavy to pronounce. I admitted to her that I knew Jay was a kind, handsome, funny, compassionate, stable companion, and yet . . .

And yet. I felt so displaced. So scared and unsupervised. Like I was going to get caught and punished for staying out past curfew, or drinking too many bottles of Pinot Grigio and having sex on the floor. I felt like I was betraying my parents by making this new life without them. Signing up for a joint bank account and calling this dusty apartment home. We lived above a jazz club that piped in Brubeck covers and fried catfish fumes. The telephone company and the mail carrier tried to convince us that our street number didn't exist. The front door was made of plywood and shook when we opened or closed it. There were nightly visits from a tribe of mice.

I hung photographs of my mother and father on every wall, then made up their running commentary of disapproval. Neither of them had ever really gotten to know Jay well. My father had died two decades before, and even I had trouble recalling the timbre of his voice. My mom had met Jay, but was ill at the time. Neither of them had ever given me their consent or support or defined this as love. I piled their copies of Dickens and Melville on our bookshelf. Hung my mother's wedding gown next to mine in the closet. Even though I was thirty years old, I still wanted my mommy and daddy to tell me what to do.

But the biggest sign to me that something was missing from our new life together was the empty space on our mantel. Juan and Martita were watching over another couple now. I longed for their steady vigil, their constant endorsement. They had been a lineage; a trust from four other couples.

We believe in your love.

We respect your differences.

We promise to stand sentinel as you commit yourselves to each other for always.

In their place I stacked magazines and unopened mail. Once in a while I filled a wedding vase with cut flowers, but in a day or two they'd be covered with a fine shimmer of soot from the busy street below. I started staying out later with friends or writing in bars. I didn't want to face Jay or that feeling of permanent absence. I didn't want to examine why I needed somebody, even an inanimate somebody, to tell me I'd made the right decision.

Meanwhile, Sarah and Nate were having some troubles of their own. Nate had been married years before, and when Sarah moved into his home, she felt like she had to step around his first wife's shadow. She didn't know how to make space for their new life together. The parallels between how Nate clung to his past and shut her out and how I was doing the same to Jay were obvious, but I managed to willfully ignore them. I told Sarah she deserved to be treated like a queen and if he couldn't commit to her completely then he was being cruel.

I didn't realize how bad it became until I got Sarah's shortest, densest e-mail.

I left.

I read it and reread it, trying to hear her voice, to smell her breath, to feel her fingers as they touched the keyboard. She'd packed up her belongings, stuffed them into her car, and was driving across country. Most likely to L.A., but maybe to stay with her mom in Oregon. She wanted to talk to me but she didn't know how. She just needed to keep driving. Away from him, from that airless house, from the life she'd thought was hers.

I was heartbroken for Sarah. I imagined her hatchback whipping up loose asphalt and shoe boxes filled with love letters. Her loneliness caught me as I walked to work or wrote in my journal. Where was she now? Paying for gas on a dusty service road? Checking into a poorly lit motel and smelling someone else's shampoo on the sheets? I carried her grief like it was my own, grumbling and gritting my teeth, drinking too much coffee in the hope that I could jolt us both awake from this bad dream.

Jay wanted to look at our wedding photos. I couldn't sit still long enough to get through an album. I knew it was cold, but I couldn't name him as my soul mate. He was just too sturdy, honest, whole. Until he wasn't. The stress of my aloofness started wearing on him. He took up cigarettes again and started looking for gyms where he could spar with a punching bag. At my urging, he and I went to couples' counseling. Our therapist made me promise to come home more in the evening so we could have some quiet time together. Jay usually cooked us big bowls of pasta that we ate in front of the TV. Reruns of crime shows where we knew the villains were people instead of doubt or regret. Even though we'd inherited the queen bed from my parents' house, more often than not we pulled off the couch pillows and fell asleep curled like a cup and saucer. Jay could easily nod off mid-sentence, especially if I scratched his back. I was grateful for his slow breath and sleep twitches. Pinned between his shoulder and the back cushion, I watched the reflections of our street's traffic on our ceiling and tried to silence my body and mind.

On one such night, tracking the headlights up our darkened wall, I realized who else was lost. Juan and Martita. Maybe in that cloud of debris kicked up by Sarah's tires. Maybe tucked into the corner of a trash can back in Chicago. Maybe split in half. Martita's blond bouffant could easily be chipped or blanketed in potato peels. Juan's dark eyes peering from beneath an empty planter or pizza box. Their glue melting in an unexpected storm. This time they were gone not just from us, but maybe from the world.

When I did hear from Sarah a few weeks later, I didn't have the heart to ask her what happened to my papier-mâché guardians. It felt too trivial and I wanted to offer my support and hear about her new home in California. She sounded exhausted, but whole. Rooming with an old friend and working in an animal shelter. Dying her hair carrot red. There were too many restraints on her when she was with Nate and she needed to see who else she could be without him.

I was relieved for her. I was relieved for me, too. As I listened to her tales of the open road, I knew for certain that I did not want that. This apartment still didn't feel entirely like home, but it was familiar. Even the plywood door reminded me that there was stability in my life that I'd never had before. That I'd never known I desired. I told Jay about the missing dolls and he agreed we should just let them go. We laughed about their buckteeth and flaky skin. We rearranged our two rooms a bit and unpacked a few more of our wedding gifts. One night, we climbed out our bedroom window, sat on the rooftop, and found the Manhattan skyline peeking through the trees.

While Sarah and Nate restarted their separate lives and Juan and Martita floated in lands unknown, Jay and I met on that rooftop night after night, as if for the first time. We didn't chat with first-date giddiness. Or make daunting promises for our future. We just stayed in that one spot, which is actually what I remember initially attracting me to him years before, back in Chicago. That he sat across the bar from me, found my eyes, and didn't let go.

I brought out a bag of potting soil, three envelopes of seeds, and a watering can. There was just a trunk-size patch of sunlight on the hot siding. Enough room for a row of small terra-cotta pots. I started with a few pansies, sunflowers and dill. We bought a tiny Weber grill and grilled chicken cutlets; a few beach chairs made our makeshift patio complete. I remember the morning I saw our first shoots peeking through the dirt.

"Look what just happened!" I pointed giddily.

"It didn't just happen. You made it happen," said Jay.

"You did, too," I corrected.

Not just because he'd taken some turns with the watering can and moved the pots to a shady edge when the June sun blazed too bright. But because he continued to be there for me, to believe in me and us and our future even if it lay inside a pile of dirt.

The pansies were bright but short-lived. The sunflower never made it past a scratchy stem, and I've yet to taste fresh dill from my own garden. But Jay and I kept tending to the plants through that first hazy summer as husband and wife. We even hosted a small dinner party on that roof—a few new friends who each climbed through our bedroom window and sat on our quilt next to the jazz club's exhaust fan, telling us it was quaint and cozy. Our new community.

And when the chill of fall drove us back indoors, we pulled off the worn cushions and lay on our couch once again. I scratched Jay's back until he sank into sleep and then I gazed into the night, focusing on streetlights and shadows. On what I had instead of what was missing. I had a faithful companion next to me. I had a front door to open and lips stained with tomato sauce. I had a packet of seeds to plant again next year. These were gifts more valuable than the stack of boxes with candlesticks, vases, frames, or figurines.

As Jay snored next to me, my breath grew slower and steadier, too. It was time to move into my life without any parents or talismans pointing the way. Time to trust in the man beside me, holding me. Time to believe in this love wholly.

Acknowledgments

First and foremost, thank you to Wendy Sherman for believing in this project from the beginning. I'm also grateful for the help of Victoria Sperling, who offered insightful comments, communicated with our contributors, and provided moral support when necessary. Special thanks to my agent friends Erin Harris for putting me in touch with the ever-talented Susan Jane Gilman, and Barbara Poelle for introducing me to Sophie Littlefield, who is a beautiful person both in life and on the page. I'd also like to acknowledge Liza Monroy, whom I've never properly thanked for introducing me to the world of writing and publishing. I owe you more than you realize. Sue Shapiro, a pillar in the New York City writing community, was a true champion of this book and a willing contributor. And a special thank-you to Ann Hood, who is a writer everyone should read, and a teacher everyone should have. I'm also thankful to the faculty of the MFA program in Creative Writing at the New School, particularly Zia Jaffrey and Jackson Taylor. Brittney Inman Canty, Suzanne Reisman, and Emily Adler were also instrumental in this entire journey, and I want them to know how much I've appreciated their help along the way.

When I was putting this anthology together, I often thought of the cabinet in which my grandfather carved his and my grandmother's initials inside a heart with an arrow through it. It's the same cabinet that holds many of the books that shaped who I am. I want to thank them, Mike and Bette London, for teaching me to love stories.

Thanks to my grandparents Nathan and Dorothy Perel as well. My grandfather once asked me who I thought his best friend was. I said I didn't know. But then he pointed toward the kitchen to where my grandmother was standing and said, "There she is." You were the inspiration behind this book.

Lastly, thank you to my brother, Greg, who always sent us cookies while we were working on this, and who is hands-down the best brother anyone could ask for. And thank you, Mom—if I could choose any mother in the world I'd pick you every time—And thank you, Dad—you will always be my hero.

—*Kim Perel*

Biggest thanks to Kim Perel, my partner in this wonderfully fun project. It all started with her vision.

Andie Avila is a great editor and a joy to work with. The project blossomed with tremendous good faith and excitement from everyone at Berkley, especially Denise Silvestro, Susan Allison, Leslie Gelbman, and our fantastic publicist Rosanne Romanello. Victoria Sperling did much of the heavy lifting and handled the abundance of details required for an anthology.

We could never have brought together such amazing writers without the help of our many editor and agent friends. Reaching out to writers we knew and some we didn't seemed like a daunting task at first, but the idea of essays on the first year of marriage really resonated. Of course the true and ultimate credit for this book goes to the women who shared their personal stories in these pages. I am honored by their generosity and no matter how many times I read these essays I continue to be moved by the heartfelt honesty, wit, and talent.

While I've been in book publishing for my entire adult life, this project was different and has given me a fresh view of how things work, namely from the author's perspective. Maybe every agent should be an author even just once to fully appreciate the experience—the mixture of anticipation and pride that comes with actually creating the book. This process has been illuminating in unexpected ways and I know I'll be a better agent for it. So many of the writers I've worked with over the years have become good friends and I sit here now even more in awe of what they do.

I am so fortunate to have incredible friends and a loving, supportive family. We've been through a lot together these past few years and yet always manage to find humor in this crazy journey. With all my love I want to thank my sweet daughters, Samantha and Alexandra. They inspire me every day.

—*Wendy Sherman*

About the Contributors

Cathy Alter is a Washington, D.C.–based writer whose articles and essays have appeared in the *Washington Post*, the *Washingtonian*, the *Atlantic*, the *Huffington Post*, and *McSweeney's*. She is the author of *Virgin Territory: Stories from the Road to Womanhood* and the memoir *Up for Renewal: What Magazines Taught Me About Love, Sex, and Starting Over*. www.cathyalter.com

Elizabeth Bard is an American journalist and author based in France. Her first book, *Lunch in Paris: A Love Story with Recipes* is a *New York Times* and international bestseller, a Barnes & Noble "Discover Great New Writers" pick, and the recipient of the 2010 Gourmand World Cookbook Award for Best First Cookbook (USA). Bard's writing on food, art, travel, and digital culture has appeared in the *New York Times*, *Wired*, *Harper's Bazaar*, and the *Huffington Post*. www.elizabethbard.com

Andrea King Collier is a journalist and author of a memoir *Still With Me...A Daughter's Journey of Love and Loss*, and *The Black Woman's Guide to Black Men's Health*. Her work has appeared in the *New York Times*, the *Washington Post*, *O, The Oprah Magazine*, *Ladies' Home Journal*, and *More*. She can be found at www.andreacollier.com

Margaret Dilloway is the author of the novels *The Care and Handling of Roses with Thorns* and *How to Be an American Housewife*. She lives in San Diego, California, with her family. She writes a blog, American Housewife, on her website: www.margaretdilloway.com

Susan Jane Gilman is the bestselling author of *Hypocrite in a Pouffy White Dress*, *Kiss My Tiara*, and *Undress Me in the Temple of Heaven*. A regular contributor to NPR, she has appeared on the *Today* show, *Men Are From Mars*, and *ABC World News Now*, and has been featured in *USA Today*, *Ms. Magazine*, *People*, and *Glamour*. She published her first piece of fiction in the *Village Voice* when she was sixteen; since then, she has won numerous literary and journalistic awards. She lives in Geneva, Switzerland, and is currently at work on a novel. Visit her website: www.susanjanegilman.com

Ann Hood is the author, most recently, of the bestselling novels *The Knitting Circle* and *The Red Thread* and the memoir *Comfort: A Journey Through Grief*, which was a *New York Times* Editors Choice and named one of the top ten nonfiction books of 2006 by *Entertainment Weekly*. A regular contributor to the *New York Times* and NPR's *The Story* with Dick Gordon, Hood has won two Pushcart Prizes, a Best American Food Writing and Best American Spiritual Writing Award. Visit her website: http://www.annhood.us

Joshilyn Jackson is the *New York Times* bestselling author of five novels, including *Gods in Alabama, Backseat Saints*, and *A Grown-Up Kind of Pretty*. She lives in quasi-rural Georgia with her husband, their two kids, and way too many feckless animals. You can visit her on the web at http://joshilynjackson.com

Jill Kargman is a *New York Times* bestselling author of trashy novels including *Momzillas, The Right Address* and *The Ex.-Mrs. Hedgefund.* Her memoir, *Sometimes I Feel Like A Nut,* is an essay collection that can be found in the humor section of your bookstore. She lives in New York. www.jillkargman.com

Sally Koslow is the author of *Slouching Toward Adulthood: Observations from the Not-So-Empty Nest* (Viking,) an examination of people in their twenties and thirties; three novels: *The Late Lamented Molly Marx, With Friends Like These* (Ballantine) and *Little Pink Slips* (Putnam), with a fourth novel in progress. She contributes essays to many magazines and has been featured in *DIRT: The Quirks, Habits, and Passions of Keeping House.* You can read Sally's work on www.sallykoslow.com

Claire LaZebnik is coauthor with Dr. Lynn Kern Koegel of two nonfiction books (*Overcoming Autism* and *Growing Up on the Spectrum*) and has published six novels, including *Families and Other Nonreturnable Gifts* and her first young adult novel, *Epic Fail.* Another YA novel, *The Trouble with Flirting,* will be out next winter. She lives in Pacific Palisades with her husband and four kids. www.clairelazebnik .com

Sophie Littlefield writes the award-winning post-apocalyptic Aftertime series for Harlequin Luna. She also writes paranormal fiction for young adults. Her first novel, *A Bad Day for Sorry,* won an Anthony Award for Best First Novel and an RT Book Award for Best First Mystery. Sophie grew up in rural Missouri and makes her home in northern California www.sophielittlefield.com

Darcie Maranich lives with her family in Tucson, Arizona, where she spends an inordinate amount of time shooing away scaly desert creatures and tweezing cactus spines from her son's extremities. Darcie blogs at www.suchthespot.com

Jenna McCarthy is the author of *If It Was Easy They'd Call the Whole Damn Thing a Honeymoon: Living with and Loving the TV-Addicted, Sex-Obsessed, Not-So-Handy Man You Married.* (Please note that it says the man *you* married, not the one she married. Her husband likes it when she points that out.) She is the author of four previous books, and her work has been published in magazines and anthologies around the world. Visit Jenna online at www.jennamccarthy.com

Liza Monroy is the author of the novel *Mexican High* and the forthcoming memoir *The Marriage Act*, which further explores her unconventional relationship with Emir. She lives in Brooklyn and teaches writing at Columbia University and elsewhere. Liza has written for the *New York Times'* Modern Love column, *The New York Times Magazine*, the *Los Angeles Times*, *Newsweek*, *Salon*, *Women's Health*, *Everyday With Rachael Ray*, the *Village Voice*, *Jane*, *Poets & Writers*, *Self*, *Bust*, *Publishers Weekly*, and others. www.lizamonroy.com

Sarah Pekkanen is the international bestselling author of three novels: *These Girls*, *Skipping a Beat*, and *The Opposite of Me*. She has also written two linked short stories available for eReaders titled "All Is Bright" and "Love, Accidentally." A former D.C. journalist who has also worked as a waitress, pet-sitter, model, babysitter, and stand-in on Hollywood films, she now lives in Chevy Chase, Maryland,

with her husband, three young sons, and rescue Lab. www.sarah
pekkanen.com

Rebecca Rasmussen is the author of the novel *The Bird Sisters* (Crown/
Random House 2011). She lives in Los Angeles, California, with her
husband and daughter, where she teaches writing at UCLA. She's been
married for six lovely years. She still favors black dresses over white ones,
and real playgrounds over ones named after the Devil. She spends her
days writing and teaching and trying to be as grateful for this wonderful
life as she can be. www.rebeccarasmussen.com

Susan Shapiro is the author of eight books, including *Unhooked*, *Speed
Shrinking*, *Overexposed*, *Lighting Up*, and the memoir *Five Men
Who Broke My Heart*, which is currently being made into a movie. She
teaches her popular "instant gratification takes too long" writing method
at the New School, NYU, and private workshops. She has written for
the *New York Times*, the *Washington Post*, the *Los Angeles Times*,
Newsweek, *The Nation*, *Salon*, *Tin House*, *Daily Beast*, the *Village
Voice*, *People*, *Psychology Today*, *More*, and *Marie Claire*. www.susan
shapiro.net

Abby Sher is a writer and performer living in Brooklyn, New York. Her
memoir, *Amen, Amen, Amen: Memoir of a Girl Who Couldn't Stop Praying (Among Other Things)* got a nod from Oprah and won the *Elle* Readers' Prize, *Chicago Tribune*'s Best of 2009, and *Moment Magazine*'s
Emerging Writers Award. Abby also wrote a young adult novel, *Kissing
Snowflakes*, which is about snowboots and stepmoms. She's written
for the *New York Times*, the *Los Angeles Times*, *Self, Jane, Elle*, and

HeeB. She is still happily married to Jay and they have two hilarious children. www.AbbySher.com

Claire Bidwell Smith is the author of *The Rules of Inheritance*, a memoir about coming of age in a fog of grief after losing both her parents at a very young age. She has written for many publications including *Time Out New York*, *Yoga Journal*, *BlackBook Magazine*, the *Huffington Post* and *Chicago Public Radio*. She lives in Los Angeles and is a therapist specializing in grief. www.clairebidwellsmith.com

Daphne Uviller is the author of the novels *Hotel No Tell* and *Super in the City*, and is the coeditor of the anthology *Only Child: Writers on the Singular Joys and Solitary Sorrows of Growing Up Solo*. She lives with her first and only husband in New York's Hudson Valley with their two children. She can be found at www.daphneuviller.com

Kristen Weber spent most of her career working in New York City book publishing, most recently as a senior editor for Penguin's New American Library, before relocating to Los Angeles in June of 2009. Now she works as an independent book editor in between relearning to drive and hanging out with her husband and her pug. Her short fiction has been published in *Girls' Life Magazine* and in *The Girls' Life Big Book of Short Stories*. You can visit her website at www.kristenweber.com

Judith Marks-White is the *Westport News* (Connecticut) award-winning columnist of "The Light Touch," which has appeared for the past twenty-six years. She is the author of two novels published by Random House/Ballantine: *Seducing Harry* and *Bachelor Degree*, which won a Reader's Prize 2009 from *Elle* magazine. Judith teaches humor writing, writes for numerous anthologies, and lectures widely. She is working on her next book. www.judithmarks-white.com

Amy Wilson is the author of *When Did I Get Like This? The Screamer, The Worrier, The Dinosaur-Chicken-Nugget Buyer, and Other Mothers I Swore I'd Never Be* (William Morrow, 2010). She is also the creator of the one-woman show *Mother Load*, which followed its hit Off-Broadway run with a national tour of sixteen cities. She blogs at whendidigetlike this.com

CREDITS

Wedding Cake for Breakfast

DISCUSSION QUESTIONS

1. The stories in this book are snapshots of life; they reveal the complicated, the funny, the sometimes challenging experiences that women face during that pivotal first year of marriage. Which of these essays resonates the most with you and why?

2. Several stories, including Joshilyn Jackson's "The Marry Boy" discuss friendship as a foundation for marriage. How important is being friends first in a romantic relationship versus having a relationship that begins with passion and attraction? How did yours begin?

3. In "Marriage Changes Things" Liza Monroy writes about her unconventional marriage to her best friend Emir: *"I had expected nothing to change. But here we were, an unconventional twosome who suddenly found ourselves filling the most conventional roles. Marriage, I thought, was not supposed to do this—not to us—but as it turns out, marriage changes things no matter what kind of couple you are."* Discuss how Susan Jane Gillman also touches on this same sentiment in her essay "Do You Want Fries with That?" and the subconscious ways people fall into certain roles in a marriage.

4. Margaret Dilloway's "Love in the Time of Camouflage" and Darcie Maranich's "All the Time in the World" deal with their experiences as army wives. In "Home Is Where the Husband Is," Kristen Weber also touches on long-distance relationships. Discuss how their husbands' time away from home affected each couple. Do you believe distance makes the heart grow fonder? Or that distance just creates more distance in the relationship?

5. In her essay "Faith and Fairy Tales," Andrea King Collier writes: *"I would have appreciated it if someone had just said that the first year of marriage is the thing you have to go through to get to the happily married part."* Is there too much focus on weddings these days and not enough on actually being married?

6. In "Animal Husbandry," Claire LaZebnik recounts how she finally realized that she could start her own traditions and break free from those she grew up with, while Elizabeth Bard's "Twinkie Au Chocolat" and Sarah Pekkanen's "Blending a Family" show ways in which family customs can be at odds in a new marriage. How do we decide what to borrow from our own upbringing and when to change it up? What are some of the customs you consciously changed in your marriage versus the ones with which you were raised?

7. Sophie Littlefield's "He Chose Me" features a marriage that ended. She discusses putting herself on a shelf for her marriage. Do you think women often do this? How important is it to maintain your own independence and identity in a marriage, and what are some ways women are able to maintain theirs?

8. Abby Sher's "Juan and Martita" and Claire Bidwell Smith's "The First Year" are both about how they navigated their respective first year of marriage without their mother (and Bidwell Smith learns she's becoming a mother). How pivotal a role do mothers play in the first year of marriage? What might they do to help the young marriage, and what should they not do?

9. Susan Shapiro, in "The Last Honeymoon," wonders what it would be like if she'd ended up with an old flame. Do you think most women go into their marriages with unanswered questions about old flames? What

kinds of "what-ifs" do you feel women generally harbor entering into marriage?

10. In "Ghosts of Husbands Past," Judith Marks-White talks about how she and her future husband arrived at the "marital altar like beasts of burden dragging behind us remnants of our past." Discuss the role that the past plays in these essays and the ways in which our past relationships color our present or future ones.

11. In both "Ciao Baggage" by Cathy Alter and "The Devil's Playground" by Rebecca Rasmussen, things go wrong, but the relationship is as strong as ever and never falters under the pressure. What things have happened in your life that have tested your relationship, and how important is it to learn how to navigate challenges as a couple?

About the Editors

Vincent Remini / Vivid

Kim Perel (right) is a New York City–based literary agent and writer. She holds an MFA degree in creative writing from the New School. She has attended more than fifteen weddings in the past year. This is her first anthology.

After a long career as a book publisher, **Wendy Sherman** (left) established her New York–based literary agency twelve years ago out of a desire to work more closely with writers, and she's loved every minute of it. She lives with her two semi-grown daughters and one very adorable King Charles Spaniel.